A PRIEST IN

A PRIEST IN GALLIPOLI

THE WAR DIARY OF FR HUGH CAMERON

JOHN WATTS

MUNGO
2015

Published in Glasgow, UK

Mungo Books, an imprint of Ovada Books

info@ovadabooks.com
ovadabooks.com

ISBN 978-1-905965-13-7

A catalogue record for this book is available from the British Library

CONTENTS

ACKNOWLEDGEMENTS

The author gratefully acknowledges the help given so readily by Donna Maguire, Archivist of the Scottish Catholic Archives, Edinburgh. I also wish to thank Fr Michael MacDonald of Ardkenneth, South Uist for kindly supplying the images of Fr Cameron, and Màiri Ceit MacKinnon of Barra who generously shared her historical knowledge of her island with me for this and a previous book. Thanks also to two of my sons, John Joseph for putting his extensive knowledge of matters military at my disposal, and Caoimhín for taming the computer.

ILLUSTRATIONS

Maps

Images

INTRODUCTION

Between September 1915 and the following July Fr Hugh Cameron, a priest of the Scottish diocese of Argyll and the Isles, kept a diary recording his experiences as an army chaplain in the First World War. He was attached to the 1st and 2nd Lovat Scouts, two regiments that formed part of the Highland Mounted Brigade and saw service in the Dardanelles and later in Egypt, Salonika and France.

A Priest in Gallipoli presents the first part of Fr Cameron's Diary, covering the period September–December 1915 when the Brigade was fighting in the Dardanelles in the ill-fated Gallipoli Campaign. To appreciate it better it will be useful to begin with a few words of introduction, concerning the diarist, the Highland regiments and in particular the Lovat Scouts, chaplains and their role in the Great War, the Gallipoli Campaign, and the writing of the Diary itself.

The Diarist

Fr Hugh Cameron was born at Inveroy in the Braes of Lochaber in 1876, the second child of Ewen Cameron and Janet Campbell. His birthplace, a small Highland Catholic community, was noted both for its long-serving parish priests – the one who baptised baby Hugh remained in the parish for more than half a century – and for the impressive crop of priests and bishops that it produced over the years. Hugh himself struggled into the world and was baptised at home on the day of his birth because it was feared that he might not live.[1] He was still an infant when his father died, whereupon his mother took him and his older sister away to begin a new life in Oban.[2]

From a young age he had thoughts of the priesthood, and at fourteen entered the national Junior Seminary at Blairs in Aberdeenshire. From there he graduated four years later to the Propaganda College in Rome, where he made a name for himself as a gifted student and was awarded the Gold Medal in Canon Law. But the delicate health that had dogged him from birth surfaced again and in 1898 he was hospitalised in Rome and forced to return to Scotland. Still set on the priesthood he was accepted by St Peter's seminary, and the following year moved to Paris to complete his training at St Sulpice. In 1900 he was ordained in Oban for his own diocese of Argyll and the Isles by Bishop George Smith.[3]

As was normal custom he spent a year or two serving his apprenticeship as a curate under experienced senior colleagues, before being given his own parish, St Mary's Griminish on the Hebridean island of Benbecula, in 1903. Five years later he was transferred to Our Lady Star of the Sea, Castlebay, Isle of Barra, at that time the second largest parish in the diocese. As well as serving half of Barra itself he also had to cover the string of small islands to the south known as the Bishops' Isles. It was a demanding post, with sea travel in all weathers, but as always he threw himself into it with enthusiasm and energy. Not only did he care for the spiritual needs of the community but, as was the way among the Highland clergy, also played a full part in its secular affairs.

He found himself involved in the latter almost from the day of his arrival. Over the previous two years crofters from the remote and precipitous island of Mingulay and landless cottars from Barra itself had 'raided' the nearby isle of Vatersay, at the time a single farm belonging to an absentee landlord, and claimed part of it as croft land for themselves. Because Vatersay lay within the parish, visiting it for monthly Mass was a natural part of the priest's work. There being no church on the long-uninhabited island, the new community were using a Mass rock known as *Am Beannachan* dating from the penal era for their services. At the time the Raiders were awaiting news of the outcome of their action. Fr Hugh let them know that he supported their cause, and they for their part promised him that if the Authorities permitted them to remain on the island they themselves would build a church there.

That June eight of them were arrested, tried and imprisoned in Edinburgh. They at once became a *cause célèbre* throughout

Scotland, and such was the public outcry that they were released within a month and an accommodation reached with the landlord in their favour. In 1913 they built the promised church on croft land gifted by one of their number.[4]

Fr Cameron also oversaw the building of a parish hall in Castlebay itself. He was by now Chairman of the Parish Council, and further afield was serving on the Education Committee as an Inverness County Councillor, involving frequent trips to the mainland. But for him as for many in the parish these things were about to be overtaken by war.

Highland Regiments and the Lovat Scouts

The Highlands and Islands are a part of Britain with a centuries-old military tradition. The great number of men from the region who have served in the British Army over many generations (wholly disproportionate to its sparse population), their courage, hardihood, *ésprit de corps*, honour and discipline, and the social conditions that fostered those qualities, are well documented and need no rehearsal here.[5]

Scottish, and later British, governments recognised the Highlander's martial prowess – their own forces having more than once themselves been on the receiving end of it – and from an early date sought to harness it for their own purposes. From the seventeenth century they had fostered the raising of Independent Companies among those clans known to be loyal to the Crown, commanded by the clan chiefs themselves, using Highlanders to tame the Highlands.[6] And later between 1739 and 1800 they had sanctioned the raising of no less than thirty Highland regiments for the British Army (twenty of which were disbanded after a few years), as well as thirty Fencible regiments raised specifically for home defence and all similarly short-lived.[7]

For many years not all Highlanders were able to enlist or take commissions in these bodies. Until the 1790s Catholics and 'non-jurant' Episcopalians (that is, those unwilling to take an oath of allegiance to the Crown, the great majority of Highland Episcopalians) were barred by law from membership of the British Army.[8] Nor indeed would they have wished to join it, since their loyalty lay with the Stewart king in exile. Not until a generation after Culloden, when it had finally become clear that there was no way back for the House of Stewart, could they with a clear conscience consider such a career.

Once these obstacles were overcome they could freely enlist, and many did. For their communities there had been a complete turnabout in attitude to the Government and its forces in just a few decades. And this was matched by a *volte face* in the attitude of the Government and public opinion regarding *them*: men whose wildness and 'disaffection' had once been feared and despised were now looked upon with admiration for their martial prowess and loyalty.[9] This admiration was to grow and these qualities to be confirmed and become a byword in numerous military actions of the Highland regiments through the nineteenth century.

One Highland Catholic army officer who served towards the end of the century and is of particular relevance here was Simon Joseph Fraser. Born in 1871, at sixteen he succeeded to the title of 16th Lord Lovat on the death of his father, inheriting the family seat at Beauly in the Eastern Highlands and an estate that reached to North Morar in the West. By nature an outdoors man, three years in the Life Guards and an expedition across Abyssinia to the Blue Nile had added experience to his natural aptitudes.

When in 1899 British troops were sent to South Africa to engage the Boers, they faced an adversary using tactics quite unfamiliar to them. Having no answer to the Boers' local knowledge of the terrain, their mobility and their hit-and-run attacks, they suffered a series of humiliating reverses. Like many others Lord Lovat realised that to survive against this elusive enemy the Army would need to change its mentality, adopt new tactics, and take on board new skills. In particular, it would need men skilled in reconnaissance, stalking and marksmanship in rough country. And he believed that just such men were already to hand among the ghillies, keepers and shepherds of the Highlands, who if given basic military training could – as he put it – help the Army 'match the Boers at their own game'.[10]

He explained his thinking to the War Office, and with their blessing raised two Companies from the Highlands in 1900, made up of men selected for their scouting skills in particular. They served in South Africa as part of the Highland Brigade, winning warm praise for their specialist expertise and conduct. After the ceasefire of 1902 they were disbanded, but resurrected the following year as Yeomanry regiments, each comprising squadrons recruited on an area basis and based and trained locally. Several of the squadrons, notably those from Lochaber and Uist, included a good proportion of Catholics. In 1908 the two regiments, now known as the 1st and 2nd Lovat Scouts, were integrated into the newly formed Highland Mounted Brigade, commanded by Lord Lovat himself.

When Britain declared war on Germany in August 1914 the Brigade was mobilised as part of the Territorial Army. For five months they were engaged mainly in coastal defence in the East of England, before being sent in April 1915 to Hunstanton in Norfolk for training for the Front line.

Like every other regiment about to enter the conflict the Scouts were looking to take on chaplains to attend to the men's spiritual needs; and since they included a good number of Catholics among the ranks and officers they would need at least one RC chaplain. Fr Hugh Cameron, who was still in Castlebay at this time, volunteered his services. One of three priests from the diocese to be commissioned in the Army that year, he joined the Scouts at their training camp at Hunstanton.

Military Chaplains and their role in the First World War

From its inception the British Army employed chaplains to care for the spiritual needs of its members. Belief in a providential God was more rooted and general than is the case in Britain today, and religious observance was mandatory with attendance at Sunday services considered a compulsory Parade. In these circumstances chaplains had an important and accepted role to play.

In the early days the Army's concept of chaplaincy was entirely English. Despite the fact that so many of its members were Scottish Presbyterian, English and Welsh Non-Conformist, or Roman Catholic, all its chaplains were Church of England. Until 1822 the Presbyterian troops were compelled to attend Anglican services, and though their own ministers were recognised for chaplaincy work from 1827 it was a dozen more years before they were officially admitted into barracks. Catholic chaplains were accepted from 1836, though at first unpaid, but celebration of the Mass was still forbidden in barracks. The Methodists had to wait until 1881 before being granted their own chaplains. It was the experience of men of all religious persuasions serving together as comrades in war, particularly in the Crimea and South Africa, that firmly cemented the principle and practice of denominational chaplains.

The importance of the chaplaincy role always rose in war time, when men were faced with the close reality of death. And in the First World War, with the quite new horrors of the trenches, it rose hugely. The number of chaplains alone tells us this: at the outbreak of the war there were a mere 117; before its end there were close to 3500.[11] Their importance was recognised by the Government and the Army's own High Command, not only in caring for the men's spiritual needs but for helping to maintain morale in often desperate circumstances.[12] Field Marshal Haig very much believed in their value: he once told them that 'a good chaplain was as valuable as a good general'.

It was a difficult task that they had, nonetheless. In the first place, they held the rank of officer – normally captain – and as such were inevitably to some extent distanced from the men. And in the case of many of the Anglican chaplains, especially, the gulf was often reinforced by an obvious difference in class. Secondly, while the troops were fighting and dying, they did not fight (though a good few died), and this made them less than admirable in some men's eyes. Thirdly, their work was only vaguely defined, and their performance of it impossible to measure. To a good extent each padre had to create his own role, and this he might interpret as anything between the strictly spiritual and the almost solely temporal. As one modern commentator has observed, 'slipping between the roles of welfare officer and priest did not come easily to many'.[13] Some sought to integrate and to employ their time profitably by making themselves useful in practical ways, in the stores, for instance, or in the Ambulance Tent. Lastly, in the face of the horrors of war many chaplains found their own faith tested to the limit, and a few even lost it entirely.

The Catholic padres were not immune from such difficulties, of course. But several contemporary eye-witness accounts suggest that their role was less ambivalent, and that the men generally accepted and looked to them more than was often the case with their colleagues from other denominations.[14] This is not to say that they were better men; rather that the set and familiar liturgies that they provided were more likely to offer men a sense of objectivity, clarity and security in times of extreme danger than improvised prayer or counsel could give. In particular, the Mass, Confession and Extreme Unction had a deep relevance for men daily facing death. And since these things were at the heart of their priestly work they were able to be what they were and what the men wanted them to be – priests.

For this reason they probably found it easier to be close to those whom they served than did some of their colleagues. And they had other advantages too. There was rarely such a class difference between them and the men as was the case with most of the Anglican padres. (In the Highland regiments, recruited locally within a close-knit society in which nearly everyone was kin or neighbour, class as generally understood had little relevance, whatever the chaplain's denomination.) The Catholic chaplains were also closer to the men in a literal sense, since they could spend as much time as they wished in the trenches, whereas those of the Church of England were restricted by military regulations to the Rear Dressing Stations.

Though such differences were real they should not be exaggerated. In the terror and trauma of the Front all the chaplains must often have struggled, all must have been tested to the utmost – physically, spiritually, in their morale and in their very faith. In that crucible each man was thrown upon himself, and his personal ability to cope put on trial. The fact that quite a large number of padres of every denomination were killed, and a good proportion decorated, suggests that many fine men were doing a difficult job courageously and well.

Fr Cameron was one of them, and he measured up better than almost all his colleagues, as we shall see. Physically he was ill equipped to do so, having never been strong from birth. But his character, his spiritual strength and his approach to the task of chaplain carried him through with honour.

The Gallipoli Campaign

The entry of Turkey into the war on the side of Germany in November 1914 had changed the balance of the conflict. The Western Front remained its main theatre, but with the Dardanelles no longer neutral the shipping route between the Black Sea and the Mediterranean was closed and Russia isolated. In London Churchill and others urged the seizure of the Gallipoli peninsula[15] in order to gain control over the Dardanelles region. At a stroke, they argued, this would re-open the line of communication, assist Britain's ally Russia and take Turkey out of the war. In January 1915 the British War Council agreed to sanction the operation, which according to the original plan was to be a naval assault only.

The attack began in mid-February. But – not for the last time – the Allies had seriously underestimated the ability of the Turks to respond. Within a month, after substantial losses including three battleships crippled, it had become clear that a solely naval operation could not succeed, and the decision was taken to give the Army the major role in the offensive. This would be led by a command staff under Sir Ian Hamilton based on the nearby island of Imbros. The troops were to be assembled at the Allies' Supplies and Communications base at the port of Mudros on the neighbouring isle of Lemnos, from where they would be landed at several points on the peninsula.

The landings finally took place on 25–26 April, the British force beaching at Helles on the Western tip of the peninsula, the Australian and New Zealand troops some sixteen miles further to the north-east at what came to be known as 'Anzac Cove', and the French at Kum Kale on the Asian side (Map 1). It was the largest amphibious operation of the war; indeed, perhaps the largest in the history of war. But again the strategy was ill suited to the reality of the conditions: the Allied forces were isolated from one another; the terrain was mountainous, affording little cover, with the Turks defending the high ground; and the five week delay had given the enemy vital time to bring in reinforcements. Though the British and Anzac troops made minor gains they rarely penetrated far beyond the narrow coastal strip, and were never able to hold the high ground of the interior or wrest it from its defenders.

In response to Hamilton's argument that with more men on the ground he could achieve his goal the War Office sanctioned five further Divisions to be sent over that summer. These were landed at Suvla Bay, closer to Anzac Cove, the intention being that they could readily link with the Australian and New Zealand forces (Map 1). But they were hardly ideal reinforcements, comprising as they did Territorials and troops of the 'New Army' recently raised under Kitchener's recruitment campaign, inadequately trained men under mainly inexperienced officers.

Thus reinforced the Allies launched a two-pronged offensive from Suvla and Anzac on 6 August. The plan was over ambitious, the British assault blunted by indecision, and the terrain

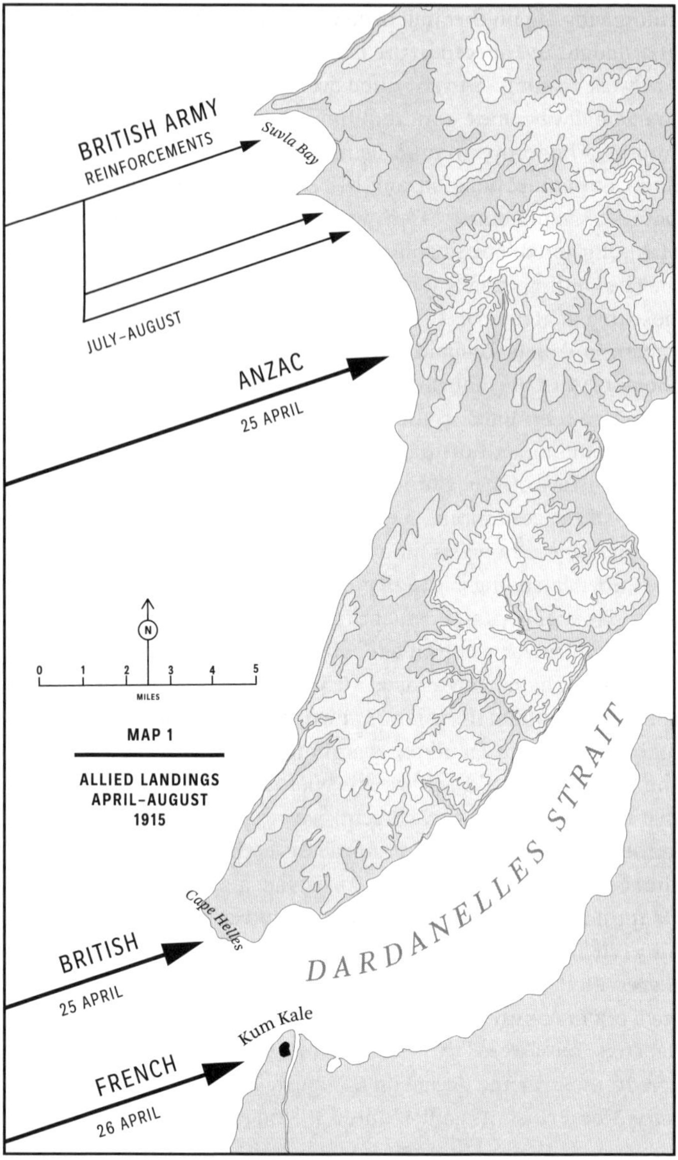
BRITISH ARMY
REINFORCEMENTS
Suvla Bay
JULY–AUGUST
ANZAC
25 APRIL
N
0
1
2
3
4
5
MILES
MAP 1
ALLIED LANDINGS
APRIL–AUGUST
1915
Cape Helles
BRITISH
25 APRIL
DARDANELLES STRAIT
Kum Kale
FRENCH
26 APRIL

unforgiving. Again the attackers were unable to secure the ridges or dislodge the Turks from the main hills.

It was now high summer, the coastal strip baking in the heat, swarming with flies and rotten with the stench of unburied corpses. Almost everyone was suffering from dysentery, and with no space for field hospitals on their narrow foothold of land there was a constant shuttle of hospital ships leaving for the safety of Malta, Egypt or home. Though the reinforcements had brought the total Allied complement on the peninsula up to some 100,000, close to half of them were now unfit for duty.

Several smaller offensives were attempted in August, all equally abortive. With the failure of the last of them on 21st it had become obvious to everyone on the ground – but apparently not to the Command Staff in the comfort of their Imbros HQ – that the chance of success was virtually nil. The Campaign had sunk into stalemate.

This was the situation when the Highland Mounted Brigade – comprising the Inverness Royal Horse Artillery, the Fife and Forfars, and the 1st and 2nd Lovat Scouts with their chaplain Fr Hugh Cameron – arrived at Suvla on 25 September. By now reports were beginning to trickle in to London from the Gallipoli front, criticising the leadership of Hamilton and his staff and accusing them of being out of touch with the reality of the trenches in their sanctuary on Imbros. Evacuations were running at over 600 every day, and it was evident that survival was now the only attainable goal.[16] But winter was not far off, an unknown that threatened to be as lethal as the summer had been. When it arrived would even survival be attainable?

Yet Hamilton still believed that victory was possible, it seemed, for early in October he was again asking for further reinforcements. But in London the government's Dardanelles Committee were losing faith in him and in the Campaign. On 14th they debated the case for withdrawal. Though split on the issue they agreed as to the Commander-in-Chief, instructing Kitchener to relieve him of his duties.

Hamilton's replacement General Sir Charles Monro made it his first task to visit the front lines personally. What he saw convinced him to recommend withdrawal, though he estimated that the operation might involve the loss of up to 40% of his troops. The War Committee, still unable to reach a decision, sent Kitchener to Gallipoli to judge the matter for himself. The Turks were now using far more effective artillery. The entry of Bulgaria into the war on the side of the Central Powers in October had opened a direct rail link from Germany to Turkey, enabling the Germans to send new, more powerful weaponry to Gallipoli, including the latest howitzers. On 22 November Kitchener cabled London recommending the evacuation of Anzac and Suvla but retaining the force at Helles (this last was in reality a mere face-saver, with no strategic purpose).

On 26-28 November winter hit: torrential rain, followed by the worst blizzard known on the peninsula in forty years, followed by sub-zero temperatures. The worst conditions were at Suvla. A watercourse known as Azmac Dere ran close by. When the rain fell flood water poured down it, bringing with it corpses, dead ponies, debris and filth. The Lovat Scouts had helped to dig a communication trench from their Brigade HQ, which crossed the Azmac Dere. Because they had experience of mountain rivers in spate they had deliberately stopped their trench just short of the watercourse and continued it above. But other troops had afterwards cut it through. With the trench some four feet lower than the bed of the Dere the flood water took its natural course, rushing down it into the Reserve Trenches and the Brigade HQ.[17] By 28th some 200 of the troops at Suvla were dead, either drowned or frozen in their saturated clothes, and 500 were suffering from severe frostbite.

The War Committee's vacillation ended on 7 December when the decision was taken to evacuate all the Allied forces except those at Helles. Since withholding advance knowledge from the enemy was crucial to the operation, and in order not to weaken the men's morale, the decision was kept from all but the higher officers. There may have been leaks, nonetheless, and certainly rumour of moves afoot was rife in the days that followed.

The withdrawal was planned to take place in stages over a week, culminating on the night of 18-19 December. It was a massive task, involving not only tens of thousands of men but 2000 vehicles, some 200 large field guns and 5000 horses, under the noses of the Turks whose trenches were often only yards away. In order to deceive the enemy the Allies had been running down their use of firearms for some days, so that the evacuation week itself might seem no different from any other. The whole thing was done by night, in silence. Fortunately the long winter nights, calm seas and morning fog all favoured the evacuees.

By the last night only a minimal rearguard remained, this honour having been given to the Highland Mounted Brigade. As they slipped silently along the empty trenches delayed-action, self-firing guns devised by the Lovat Scouts went off, giving the impression that fighting men remained. The very last to leave were the Lovat Scouts themselves and a detachment of Gurkhas.

Ironically, after the naïve and maladroit handling of the Campaign, the withdrawal itself was textbook. Only in the light of day, when the mist lifted, did the Turks find themselves without an enemy. The Anzacs had suffered only two minor casualties, the troops at Suvla not a single man wounded.

The various brigades were taken to the Allies' naval base at Mudros, which became a vast entrepôt where the human cargo (or at least those who were fit for service) awaited transhipment to other war fronts. The 1st and 2nd Lovat Scouts and their comrades of the Highland Mounted Brigade were sent to Egypt, reaching Alexandria before the end of the month. But Fr Cameron did not travel with them. He had pushed himself to the limit in the trenches and his health had finally broken. On 10 December, just two days before the first evacuations, he had collapsed with severe pleurisy. He was at once put on board a hospital ship and taken first to Mudros and thence to Malta.

Four Allied divisions remained to hold Helles. But the Turks still had their twenty-one divisions on the peninsula, and these they could now concentrate on the hugely outnumbered British force. Its position was utterly untenable. Within ten days the inevitable decision was taken to evacuate. The withdrawal was effected on 8 January, using the same tactics as at Anzac and Suvla and, despite less favourable weather, with almost as few casualties.

Fr Cameron spent the first six weeks of 1916 convalescing. During that time further sea journeys took him from Malta via Sicily and Naples to Rome, and then by the same route back to Malta and finally to Egypt, where on 22 February he resumed his duties with the Lovat Scouts. In June he successfully applied for home leave, and set sail from Alexandria aboard a passenger liner early in July. The final entry in his War Diary, dated 9 July, records him passing Corsica en route to Britain.

The Subsequent Career of Fr Cameron

Early in the autumn he returned to Egypt. But his stay there was brief, for in October the Lovat Scouts were transferred to Salonika to join the Allies' Macedonia Campaign. They would serve there with distinction for the next twenty months, seeing action first against the Bulgarian forces and later against the Turks.[18]

At home Bishop George Smith of Argyll and the Isles was in his mid-seventies and visibly declining. So concerned were the Canons of the diocesan Chapter that in March 1917 they sent a report to Rome advising that he was now unfit to discharge his episcopal duties and that there was no reasonable hope of his returning to health. They requested that a co-adjutor be appointed (that is, an assistant bishop with automatic succession), adding their own three recommended names for the post. Among these was Hugh Cameron.[19] Following further communication with the Chapter's representative Rome nominated Fr Cameron as its preferred choice.

The nomination showed his high standing in the Highland Church. And at forty-one he was a good age for the mitre – old enough to have gained a wealth of experience yet young enough to offer the promise of many years' service. But Fr Hugh had no wish for it. Very probably his motive was not so much an aversion to the post as a deep attachment and loyalty to the Lovat Scouts and a wish to continue as their chaplain, at least while the war lasted.[20] Such 'family' loyalty was typical of the Scouts, typical of the Highlands, typical of the man himself, and furthermore had been forged in the crucible of Gallipoli.

Receiving the news at his base in Salonika he travelled at once to Rome and secured a personal interview with Benedict XV, in which he requested to be excused. A story has gained currency, which to my best knowledge cannot be verified and I am inclined to think apocryphal, that as his main argument he pled insanity in the family. Whatever the course of the discussion between the two men, the pope granted his wish.

In June 1918 the Commander-in-Chief of the British forces on the Western Front, Sir Douglas Haig, ordered the Lovat Scouts to be transferred to France. With the arrival of American troops in Europe the balance of the war was now tipping in the Allies' favour. In the autumn first the Bulgarians and then the Turks agreed to an armistice, and finally on 11 November, two days after the abdication of Kaiser Wilhelm, the fighting ceased.

With the return of peace the British Army's Territorial forces were disbanded, in the case of the Lovat Scouts in April 1919. Fr Cameron returned to his parish on Barra. In the same month Donald Martin was nominated bishop of Argyll and the Isles and consecrated that July, Fr Cameron being appointed his Vicar-General.

In this senior role Fr Hugh was able to play a crucial part in steadying the diocese, in particular in helping to set it on a sound financial footing and in assisting its poorest parishes. His work was gratefully recognised both in Oban and in Rome. In 1920 he was made a Canon of the Chapter, and later Provost and Domestic Prelate (the last a personal papal appointment).

In 1921 he was moved to the parish of St Andrew's Rothesay on the Isle of Bute. Unlike Barra this was not a traditional hub of the Catholic faith, but the town and its Catholic community had grown greatly over the past forty years with the arrival of new families from Glasgow and Inverclyde. Its mid-nineteenth century chapel was no longer adequate for the numbers, and through the generosity of the 4th Marquis of Bute a fine new church was already at the planning stage. Fr Hugh saw it to completion, and officiated at its opening by Bishop Martin in 1925.

He was now close to fifty and, never robust and still not wholly over the war, feeling the weight of his duties in parish and diocese. In 1926 he relinquished his post as Vicar–General, and two years later was moved to the less onerous parish of Laggan and Kingussie on the far eastern edge of the diocese.

The upland district of Laggan had supported a thriving Catholic population for the past two hundred years, and it was here that the old church was sited. But outward migration typical of the Highlands had reduced its congregation almost to nothing, while the nearby villages down in broad Strathspey had been growing proportionately. The nearest of these were Newtonmore and Kingussie, where the parish's future clearly lay. Already before Fr Cameron arrived and took lodgings in Kingussie fundraising had begun for a new church in the village. He moved the project forward and took it to the advanced planning stage. Our Lady of the Rosary and St Columba's was set to be the third church to be built by this ever-busy, ever-practical man. It was completed in spring 1932 and consecrated that July.

But Fr Hugh had not lived to see it. In the winter of 1930-31 his landlady had been touring in Italy. In the February he had met up with her in Florence and they had journeyed on to Rome, where both of them took ill. On 5 March she died, and on the same day he was admitted to hospital with severe pneumonia. But his lungs

1. Fr Cameron (centre) standing with other priests recently ordained for the diocese beside Bishop George Smith. The two priests are Fr Patrick MacDonald (left) and Fr Donald MacIntyre.

2. Fr Cameron seated centre with First Communicants in his parish of St Andrew's Rothesay, 1925 or 1926. His face shows his obvious pleasure in the occasion, in contrast to that of the rather grim nun. The other priest is Fr Duncan MacLean.

had never recovered from Gallipoli, and the illness already had too strong a grip. Nothing could be done. He declined rapidly and was dead within three days, the Rector of the Scots College at his bedside. He was buried in the College's cemetery nearby.

The Diary

Fr Cameron's War Diary is kept among the holdings of the Diocese of Argyll and the Isles (catalogue no. DA 9.47), which are at present housed in the Scottish Catholic Archives in Edinburgh. It comprises a daily record of his experiences between 5 September 1915 and 9 July 1916, and covers the period from his leaving the Hunstanton military base for Gallipoli to his sea journey back to Britain on home leave. It was written in pencil in a 1915 pocket Diary measuring a mere 85 mm x 135 mm, in which each day was allotted a single page. When he reached the new year of 1916 he used the pages at the beginning of 1915, keeping the date but moving the day forward by one day (by two from 1 March, since 1916 was a leap year). The little volume included a few blank pages at the end for 'Memoranda', and these he used from time to time to jot down his impressions and thoughts of the Campaign.

Constrained as he was by the page size he made the most of what he had by writing in a very small hand. This allowed him more scope, but it has hardly helped the task of transcription, the more so since his handwriting was poor and his punctuation erratic, (pardonable faults, for he was often writing on his knee or under fire). I have transcribed the text as he wrote it, retaining his errors and omissions, but for the sake of clarity have separated his sentences with a space where his lack of a punctuation mark has run them together. Very rarely it has been impossible to decipher his script, even with the help of others: in these cases illegible words are indicated by [   ], with or without a best guess.

The present volume does not include the whole Diary but only the first part of it, from 5 September when he was preparing to leave for Gallipoli to 13 December when he was invalided out from

Mudros. Thereafter, the accounts of his convalescence, sea journeys and subsequent posting in Egypt are of less interest, and are not included here. His Impressions, on the other hand, add much to the account and rightly find a place.

The Diary entries for 6–26 September record his sea journey from Britain to Suvla (Map 2 on p. 28), but the whole text thereafter to 10 December covers his time in the trenches in the midst of the fighting. He did not witness the entire Campaign, of course. He had not arrived when the Allies first landed, nor when the spring and August offensives took place. And he missed the evacuation, having been invalided out just days earlier. The period he recorded was the stalemate phase.

This does not make his narrative less interesting or significant, however. Indeed, in a sense the opposite is true. For whereas the Allies' early offensives and final withdrawal have been thoroughly recorded in the standard accounts of the Gallipoli Campaign, the period of stalemate has often been only cursorily mentioned. And those historians who do give a full coverage of this phase are in the main interested in the hardening attitude to the Campaign by the Government and War Cabinet in Britain. Little is said of the situation at the Front. Fr Cameron's Diary does precisely this, and is thus one of the few witness accounts that helps fill out the picture. Nor should stalemate be taken to imply stasis. Those ten weeks saw continual change – in the conditions on the ground, in morale and in purpose – change whose direction was almost all one-way, with an inevitability to it.

The diarist also differed from nearly every other eye-witness in that he wrote from the point of view of a chaplain, with interests and perspectives particular to his work. As a Catholic padre he was in the rare position of being able to mix freely and closely with both officers and men, and as the situation worsened to be privy to their changing moods and to record them along with his own.

His Diary in fact makes reference to many of the events and themes of the Campaign and of chaplaincy touched on in this

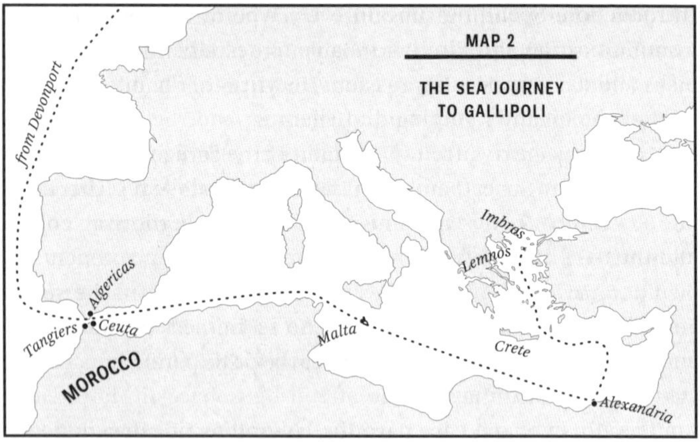

3. SS Sarnia unloading troops into Lighters for landing at Suvla Bay. It was from the Sarnia that the Lovat Scouts and Fr Cameron were landed in this way on 26 September 1915. Originally built as a passenger ship in 1910 she was taken over and adapted by the Royal Navy as an Armed Boarding Steamer in 1914. Sent to the Dardanelles in 1915, she was used to transport troops from the Allies' base at Mudros to the Fronts. After the evacuation she remained at Mudros before being transferred to Alexandria in 1917. In September 1918 she was torpedoed and sunk near Port Said with the loss of 53 men.

Introduction. Spending time in every type of trench – Reserve, Communication and Fire – he is able to describe the conditions, tasks and dangers peculiar to each. He writes of the different hazards of the enemy's sniping and shelling, and their later use of more effective heavy artillery. He tells of the ravages of dysentery after the summer heat, and then the killer floods and blizzards of late November. He describes his own work, the freedom he enjoys and the need to a large extent to create his own role and plan his own day. He gives priority above all else to the spiritual, pastoral and sacramental, but also finds time to assist in the medical tents and elsewhere. He has great admiration for the undemonstrative staunch faith of the men, who attend his services in far greater numbers than is the case with his colleagues of other denominations; he is struck by their piety in the face of death; they are his greatest consolation, and he is happiest when among them in the firing line. But he is grieved by the effect that the worsening conditions and the waste of life are having upon many: their best defence is a healthy cynicism and trench humour, some of which he quotes, but there is a creeping demoralisation as the hopelessness of their position becomes ever clearer. In some other regiments there is a noticeable loss of self-respect. The chaplains too are affected, and some find it impossible to keep a balance in their lives. Several react by 'hiding'; a few by a reckless disregard for their own safety; one or two get themselves invalided out with dubious ailments. Fr Cameron copes better than most, and latterly finds himself ministering to several regiments as well as his own. But he also struggles, and this too he records. As December approaches he notes that rumours of evacuation are rife; apparently he has even heard specific plans for how it will be effected. Finally, when he is invalided out just days ahead of the men, he admits his relief but also his feelings of guilt at leaving them.

Fr Cameron clearly believed that his record of Gallipoli was of importance and worth keeping. Fearing that he might not survive, whether through disease or a Turkish bullet, he was determined that *it* would at least. In his entry of 9 December, the day before his collapse, he wrote of his plan to hand it over to one of those being invalided out, with instructions that it be safely delivered to a priest friend in the Highlands. As things turned out, of course, he was among the invalids on the next ship and so was able to bring it home himself. I believe that his care for its preservation and his confidence in its value were justified.

Though he could not quite hold out until the general evacuation, he remained longer than nearly all his colleagues and was one of the last Catholic chaplains to leave Suvla. And this despite his far-from-robust constitution. As he himself had recognised early on, 'it is not strength and muscle but moral staying power that counts in this business'.[21] It was his personal qualities that saw him through. Years later, in an obituary to him, a friend wrote of his 'keen bright mind', his 'intrepid courage' and 'fearless frankness', his 'clear-cut practical' nature and sense of humour.[22] These qualities he carried through life, and they came to the fore at Gallipoli where they were put to their greatest test. Along with his deep faith they helped him to survive, to hold his nerve, to see if possible beyond the present horror, and still to care for others. They show through continuously in the Diary, and colour its pages. On 21 November, though already 'about played out and sick of this hopeless struggle', he promised himself that he would 'try to carry on until I drop'. And that is precisely what he did.

The Impressions

His Impressions of the Campaign, jotted down at the back of the Diary, run to somewhat over 1000 words. By internal evidence we can deduce that he recorded his ideas on four different occasions: the first on 6 November (which unaccountably he dated 6 October), the second on 12 November, the third near the end of the month, and the last on 9 December, the day before he collapsed.

The themes that dominated his thinking were the heroic fortitude of the men and some officers, the ineptitude of High Command in the safety and comfort of their headquarters, and the sinful waste of life and pointlessness of the Campaign.

How do these on-the-spot judgments compare with those of historians of Gallipoli, who have all the accumulated evidence at their disposal with which to make a measured assessment with the clarity of distance? In fact, attitudes to the Campaign have fluctuated over the years. In the immediate aftermath, failure and national humiliation prompted wholesale condemnation. Later, the published works of influential participants – notably Churchill, who had always been the prime protagonist of the venture – went some way to reinstating both its justification in principle and the strategies adopted by the Imbros Command staff. Their argument was strengthened by the publication of internal documents of the Turkish Command, which revealed how close the Allies had come more than once to breaking through.[23]

Recent historians, nonetheless, are generally highly critical of the leadership in both Imbros and London. One of their fiercest critics, Peter Hart, castigates Gallipoli as 'a lunacy that never could have succeeded, an idiocy generated by muddled thinking', 'the most doomed, the most pointless' of all the campaigns of the Great War, a 'Quixotic' adventure undertaken with a 'cavalier disregard for the elementary principles of war'.[24]

On the other hand, the courage of the men and many of the officers in the front line, always cheerful and often heroic, has become the stuff of legend. The figures speak for themselves: Gallipoli produced thirty-nine VCs, the highest number from any of the theatres of the War outside the Western Front.[25]

The stark contrast between those in High Command and those in the firing line draws the following conclusion from the author of what is perhaps the best of all accounts of the Campaign: Gallipoli, he writes, was 'the war that got away from its handlers, a tale of all that is fine and all that is foolish in the human condition'.[26] Our diarist could not know the problems and constraints faced by the decision makers, of course. In general, nonetheless, it can be said that both his unstinting praise of the fine and his withering critique of the foolish have been amply vindicated by the verdict of history.

Endnotes

1. Hugh was born and baptised on 20.4.1876 – Register of Baptisms, St Margaret's Roybridge, MP 75/1/1/2, Scottish Catholic Archives (SCA).
2. Much of the rest of the present account is based on Fr Cameron's Obituary in the *Scottish Catholic Directory* (*SCD*) 1932, 326 ff.
3. Records of Ordinations, *SCD* 1901, 274.
4. The present account based on Buxton, B. *The Vatersay Raiders* (Birlinn 2008) especially chapters 5–6 and 160 ff; and Màiri Ceit MacKinnon statement to the author.
5. One of the earliest, and best, summaries may be found in Stewart D. of Garth *Sketches of the Character, Manners and Present State of the Highlanders of Scotland, with Details of the Military Service of the Highland Regiments*, (2 vols; Archibald Constable & Co 1822) vol. 1, espec. Part I sections ii–iii and Part II section i. For a modern account, cf. e.g. Henderson D. M. *Highland Soldier, a Social Study of the Highland Regiments* (John Donald 1989) chap. 1 'Historical Introduction', especially 3–5.
6. For a detailed account see Simpson P. *The Independent Highland Companies 1603–1760* (John Donald 1996).
7. cf. Adam F. *The Clans, Septs and Regiments of the Scottish Highlands* (Famedram Publishers 8th rev. ed. Ellon 2004, first pub. W. & A. K. Johnston 1908). Adam furnishes a short account of each of the regiments, including their history (443–477), and a list of the Fencible regiments with dates (477 f). The ten regiments that proved long-lasting were the British Royal Highland Regiment (the Black Watch) (1739), the Highland Light Infantry (1777), the Seaforth Highlanders (1778), the Perthshire Highlanders (1780), the Highland Regiment of Foot (1787), the Ross-shire Buffs (later absorbed into the Seaforths) (1793), the Cameron Highlanders (1793), the Gordon

Highlanders (1794), the Argyllshire Highlanders (1794) and the Sutherland Highlanders (1800).

8. New laws ending the prohibition were enacted for the non-jurant Episcopalians in 1792 and for the Catholics the following year (32 Geo III cap. 63 and 33 Geo III cap. 44 respectively). The previous laws had been enforced strictly in the case of commissioned officers, but far less so for the rank and file.

9. As a slight caveat, there is evidence that in the nineteenth century a conscious anti-Catholic recruiting policy operated in some of the Highland regiments – cf. Henderson D. M. op. cit., 218.

10. Cf. Melville M. L. ed. *The Story of the Lovat Scouts 1900–1980* (Librario Publishing 2004) especially 22 ff. Much of the following paragraphs is based on this source.

11. In November 1918 the precise figure was 3475. These included 649 RC chaplains, some 19 percent of the total.

12. In some cases, also, padres as it were gave 'professional' affirmation to the official line that to fight the enemy was to do God's work.

13. Holmes R. *Tommy – the British Soldier on the Western Front 1916–1918* (Harper Perennial 1996, 2004 ed.) 517, in chap. 6 'Heart and Soul'.

14. Louden S. H. *Chaplains in Conflict: The Role of Army Chaplains since 1914* (Avon Books 1996) 51. Much of the previous and present paragraphs is based on this source.

15. In Turkish *Gelibolu.*

16. cf. Hart P. *Gallipoli* (Profile Books 2011, 2013 ed.) 390.

17. Based on the account of Col. Iain M. Campbell of the Lovat Scouts, in Melville M.L. op. cit., 68.

18. The fact that one fifth of their number were decorated in the Campaign reflects the high regard in which they were held – cf. Melville M.L. op. cit., 92 ff.

19. Minutes of diocesan Chapter meetings of 6. 3. 1917 & 11. 4. 1917, in Watts J. *A Record of Generous People – a History of the Catholic Church in Argyll and the Isles* (Mungo Books 2013) 168 f.

20. This certainly was the view of one respected historian of the Highland Catholic Church, the late Mgr Roddy MacDonald, who had the benefit of at least second-hand verbal witnesses.
21. *Diary*, 17 October 1915.
22. Fr Hugh Cameron obituary, *SCD* 1932, 326 ff.
23. For an excellent brief account of this change in attitude see Moorhead A. *Gallipoli* (Harper Perennial 1956, 1997 ed.) 304 ff.
24. Hart P. op. cit., 1 f.
25. Cf. Snelling S. *VCs of the First World War – Gallipoli* (Sutton Publishing 1995, 1999 ed.). Snelling's book includes biographical sketches of every recipient.
26. Carlyon L.A. *Gallipoli* (Pan Macmillan Australia 2001, Bantam 2003 ed.) 643.

Abbreviations Used in the Diary

AC	Assault Craft
ADS	Advanced Dressing Station
ASC	Army Service Corps
BHQ	Brigade Headquarters
CCS	Casualty Clearing Station
CF	Chaplain to the Forces
Communication T	Communication Trench
D Officer	Duty Officer
DS	Dressing Station
Dys	Dysentery
FA	Field Ambulance
FDS	Field Dressing Station
F&F	Fife and Forfar
FFL	Front Firing Line
HC	Holy Communion
HE	High Explosive
HMB	Highland Mounted Brigade
LS	Lovat Scouts
1LS	1st Regiment, Lovat Scouts
2 LS	2nd Regiment Lovat Scouts
L Sacrament	Last Sacrament (Extreme Unction)
2nd M Division	2nd Mounted Division
Med Ins	Medical Inspection
MG	Machine Gun
MO	Medical Officer
OC	Officer Commanding
RAMC	Royal Army Medical Corps
REs	Royal Engineers
RFA	Regimental Field Ambulance
RMO	Regimental Medical Officer
SH	Scottish Horse Regiments
T	Turkish

TURKISH WORDS USED IN THE DIARY

As in Diary	As in Turkish	English meaning
Bair	*Bayır*	*slope*
Dere	*Dere*	*shallow valley*
Sari	*Sarı*	*yellow*
Tepe	*Tepe*	*hill*

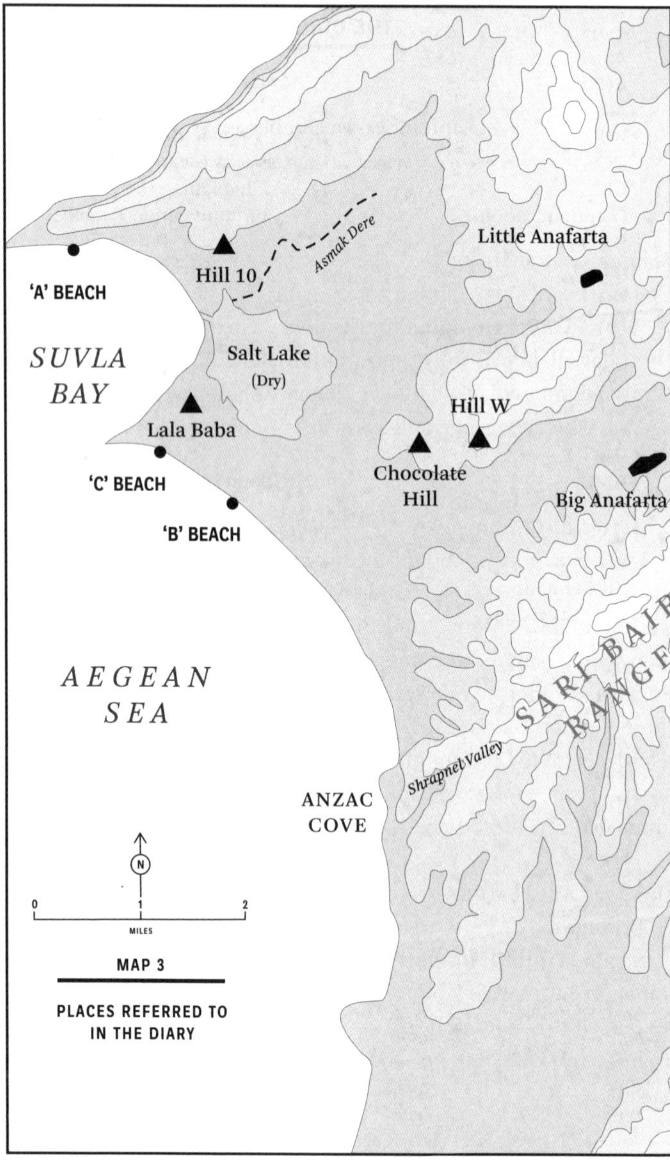

MAP 3

PLACES REFERRED TO IN THE DIARY

THE DIARY

September–December 1915

Places referred to in the Diary may be located on Map 3

Sunday SEPTEMBER 5

Here begins my War diary.

We had orders to fit out for the boat Great excitement &c.

Today all men at Holy Communion. Benediction a sight Church crammed God knows when we shall have Benediction again & where. Lots at Confession after Bened.

Monday SEPTEMBER 6

Left Hunstanton

We leave this evening for the boat where we don't know but likely Dardanelles. First train in which I was left at 5.30 pm rest in 4 other trains at intervals of 2 hours. Scene at station dreadful, so many women about weeping & wailing none over me thank God. Roberts[1] & I got into one carriage Archie Cameron stepped in & the ass left his revolver fully loaded in the rack. Roberts took it up & fooled with it It went off & shot passed a foot from me Lucky omen! We are going west somewhere. Have passed Oxford but it is funny not knowing where. However it doesnt matter.

Tuesday SEPTEMBER 7

Devonport

Steamed into Devonport dockyard at 5am, alongside our transport a Cunarder Andania Roberts & I secured a stateroom for ourselves two lucky beggars, 3 & 4 in others. Ensuite We got leave from D Officer to go ashore into town. Knocked about deu-

1. Dr Thomas Roberts was the Medical Officer of the Lovat Scouts.

ced hot & uninteresting. Got back & found rest had arrived & were being stowed away. Whole brigade travel in same ship.[1] Very comfortable for officers. Men pretty cramped. All gathered at dinner in saloon. Devonport looked very beautiful crowded with all kinds of craft. One torpedo destroyer went quite near us. Turned into our beds & slept heavily

Wednesday SEPTEMBER 8

Left Devonport

About 6am was awakened by the swish of water & the first throb of the ships engines. Got out on deck in pyjamas & found everyone else pouring out to have a last look at old England Crossed the bar & destroyers closed in on either bow. Parting very quiet. No demonstration the land soon fell behind us & we were soon in open sea. The weather is grand & the sea smooth promising a pleasant voyage. Things getting ship shape aboard

Attached to Head Q mess in company with Col. Major Grant,[2] Pocock[3] Adjt, MO & self. Quite a nice party. About 3pm our escort ran up alongside crews up on deck cheering away. Nelsons flag signal flying England expects swerved round & headed for home. That was our goodbye

Thursday SEPTEMBER 9

At Sea

Out of sight of land. Said Mass this morning in the library a small room, too small Two at HC Cols Stirling & Macdonald.[4]

1. The Highland Mounted Brigade, comprising the 1st and 2nd Lovat Scouts and the Fife and Forfar Yeomanry.

2. Either Major Forsyth Grant, 2nd Lovat Scouts, or Major Ewen Grant of Glenmoriston, 1st Lovat Scouts.

3. H. Pocock, Regimental Quartermaster. Sometimes spelled 'Pococke' in Diary.

4. Lt Col Archie Stirling, CO 2nd Lovat Scouts, and Lt Col Willie MacDonald, CO 1st Lovat Scouts.

After breakfast I interviewed the 2nd Steward an RC & got him to arrange to let me have the use of the 3rd Class Smoking Room now used as Sergeants Room at 6am every morning. That is alright

Began to go round the men taking them in rotation of Regts & Squadrons

Weather getting warmer but we seem to be heading west to judge from the time variation. Our watches gaining time. Had what is called a boat drill   Blast of ships syrene continuously   All rush on deck each with a life belt on & muster up in squadrons opposite our boats until CO comes

Friday SEPTEMBER 10

At Sea

Mass this morning in Smoking Room of Sergt Mess a fine gathering lots at Communion. Boat drill again. Think if we have to take to the boats I shall patiently wait & take to the sea for I fancy these boats will be death traps in launching. Chasing around after my men & getting them in the evening for confessions in the Col's cabin which he very kindly put at my disposal   He is a top hole man & one would do anything for him. He & Kennedy are always confabbing. K is a most detestable fellow & a rotten Catholic He is the one man in my pack who hasn't been.[1] I do dislike him.

Saturday SEPTEMBER 11

Gibraltar

Numbers at Mass & Holy Communion very steadily on the increase   The other two Padres have taken notes & are trying to copy me but with no success.

We passed through the straits of Gib in the dark. One could just see the search lights from the Rock & on the left the lit up

1. i.e. to Confession? Or even Mass? Or is there a word (such as 'co-operative') omitted here?

town of Algericas Ceuta opposite on the African coast then Tangiers brilliantly illuminated. A lovely scene A patrol boat flashed by us in the dark & ordered us to proceed so we wont have a chance to land our carefully written bundle of letters A bit rotten that we haven't had a chance of seeing the fortress in the daytime.

Sunday SEPTEMBER 12

In the Mediterranean

Mass this morning at 6.30 & at 8am. Lots at Holy Communion A few words only Hymns & singing very good. These are precious days for the men the last a good many will get for some time in all likelihood all [ ]. We are hugging the African coast

A Greek steamer passed us & signalled to us to stop but Capt carried on It was afterwards rumoured that she was a decoy leading a submarine. Submarine reported 10 miles ahead. Everybody on the qui vive. What a mess if we were hit.

Monday SEPTEMBER 13

Still running along the coast We passed Morocco today. The machine gun boys are having a high old time of it letting off at any suspicious objects but everything to them seems suspicious & they blaze away at floating boxes. Some good marinership but most of it rotten. The crowd at Mass & Communion is still maintained. Nearly all have been in & some a great many times. Protestant commentary but qu'importe! Kennedy still remains his sulky self. His brother whom I discovered in 2nd LS is a nice frank boy.

Tuesday SEPTEMBER 14

Gozo

This evening after turning a headland we sighted Malta & towards evening we anchored off the island of Gozo at a place just outside of Valetta called St Pauls Bay. It was here that St Paul was wrecked on his way to Rome as a prisoner & I could see the place described by him where two seas meet a channel separating the small island of Gozo from the main isle called in the Vulgate[1] Melita. It was a beautiful scene. The white houses rising in tiers from the water. Lots of convents evidently. We could distinguish a lot of nuns.

Wednesday SEPTEMBER 15

Malta

At Mass this morning I read the chapter of Acts[2] which describes St Pauls shipwreck & landing on the very spot we are in. Immediately after Mass we moved into the harbour of Valetta Crowded with shipping. Went ashore in a kind of gondola rowed by a puntist Maltese boys diving after silver coins Roberts & [sic] nosed round got a Servite Father & got into a jewellers shop where I bought a small pyx[3]

Afterwards bought a lot of Maltese lace sent some to Kate, Lizzie & Mrs Roberts. Got in some Italian & French Swarms of priests Capuchin[4] came on board begging from the boys Got aboard to find Archbishop Camana waiting for me with Col & Brigadier Very pleasant & dignified. He is a great gun here.

Thursday SEPTEMBER 16

At sea

We left Malta yesterday I cant say I liked it. The churches are appallingly dirty. The streets swarm with monks, priests & monsignors all evidently on the make. The Chapel of the Knights interested me & the armoury of old weapons guns &c used by the

1. The early 5th c. Latin translation of the Bible, mainly the work of St Jerome.

2. The New Testament book the Acts of the Apostles.

3. A small metal container, shaped like a pill box and with lid, used for carrying Communion hosts.

4. The Capuchins are one of the three main branches of the 1st Order of St Francis, the others being the Friars Minor and the Friars Minor Conventual. The Order itself dates from 1209, the Capuchins from 1525.

famous order of St John.[1] I don't envy Camana his job. Still he is the right man for it. Have written lots of letters to Bar[2] during the voyage all descriptive. Men are a bit bilious today after gorging on fruit yesterday bought from the bumboats.[3] The heat is great

Friday SEPTEMBER 17

At sea

We passed shoals of flying fish first I have ever seen There was a report when leaving Malta that a transport which had gone before us had been torpedoed. Hence we all must carry our life belts about with us everywhere & this morning I said Mass with one perched just where the bell should be. Heat is getting heavier. We are bound for Alexandria which we shall make tomorrow. Shoals of flying fish about pitching themselves out of the water & slithering along I thought they were birds at first

Saturday SEPTEMBER 18

At Alexandria

Awoke at day break to discover right ahead the towers & minarets of Alexandria. It was a most exquisite scene as viewed from the deck. The long low grey African coast stretched on either side the harbour. The ancient city a medley dazzling white in the glorious morning air set in a background of palms, & behind it all the most most beautiful dawn I have yet seen. It was a dreamy scene. An hour or two later the dream vanished & we woke to the reality of Alexandria hard against the coal wharf crowded with a motley throng of semi & wholly naked Arabs, all begging. A native policeman in Khaki ran here & there laying on hard with a cudgel.

1. The military Order of the Hospitallers of St John of Jerusalem, founded *c.* 1113, to care for the poor and strangers in the Holy Land, and to provide armed protection for pilgrims. Soon after the fall of Jerusalem they took refuge on Rhodes, and from 1522 in Malta.

2. Fr James Barry, parish priest of St Mun's Ballachulish in Fr Cameron's diocese, and a good friend. Referred to several times in the Diary.

3. Small boats used for bringing provisions out to ships at anchor.

Sunday SEPTEMBER 19

Alexandria

Mass this morning a fiasco attended by three or four because there was a route march at 5am which after all did not come off & I wasn't informed. Mad about it. Went ashore yesterday also today with Tommy[1] who was in a rotten restless mood. Funny chap. Took Ian Tillar off to see his cousin & had lunch there quite a [ ]. Afterwards went to Union Club the rendezvous of officers. Poor Ian a decent chap but a bit of a baby. Alexandria an awful hole near docks but some decent streets in foreign quarter all French names. Some French women too touting. Looked a rotten lot. Hear no English are allowed to trade there.

Monday SEPTEMBER 20

Alexandria

Went out again today & visited a lot of delightful French nuns Franciscans[2] who had such a nice school & orphanage. Padre Ross with me. Had to talk French & Italian & quite enjoyed it. Great fun. Afterwards at Union Club met Fr Starker whom I met once in London & who acted as Chaplain to the Munsters. He was in the first Suvla landing.[3] He was in great form & we had a topping lunch. He is dying to get back to the Peninsula not many like him in that respect. We leave Alexandria tonight for Gallipoli calling at Lemnos. Weather very hot

Tuesday SEPTEMBER 21

At Sea

We now know our destination & that is Gallipoli. We left very early this morning after having put ashore all our saddles &c We go out as infantry & are being served out with infantry equipment & webbing, which consists mainly of a most infernal pack which

1. Dr Thomas Roberts (cf. note 1, p 37).

2. These female Franciscans belonged to congregations of the Franciscan Third Order Regular.

3. In late July/early August.

one has to humph.[1] We are steering a funny course NE for fear of submarines & life belts are de rigeur. You have to carry them everywhere.

At Alexandria I met a charming old Christian Brother[2] a Londoner called Brother Felix who knew the port well having lived there some

Wednesday SEPTEMBER 22

At Sea

30 years. He was rather pessimistic about the venture in Gallipoli thought we should never get through. He was also death on the Greeks for whom his vocabulary wasnt enough. Gallipoli is evidently a hot shop (It is that! HC Nov 16)

Weather is getting perceptibly cooler as we go Northwards. We sighted the island of Crete in the afternoon, & passed a large Hospital ship coming south. Wonder if it shall be my fate to come back that way if at all! Tomorrow we make Lemnos the base of transhipment to Gallipoli Had a "serape" from a Capucin from Manchester at Alexandria

Thursday SEPTEMBER 23

Woke up to find ourselves entering the harbour of Lemnos, a magnificent anchorage quite land locked & there was a huge fleet of all classes & nationalities This island was actually looked

1. The Highland Mounted Brigade were converted into an infantry Brigade for service in Gallipoli, where a mounted Brigade would have been useless on account of the terrain.

2. The Christian Brothers were founded by Bl. Edmund Rice in Ireland in 1802 to provide education for the young. They later also founded schools in Australia, New Zealand and North and South America. A quite distinct religious Congregation of the same name (also known as the De La Salle Brothers) were founded by St Jean Baptiste de la Salle in France for a similar purpose.

on as belonging to Greece since the Balkan War[1] but when the present war broke out it was discovered that it had never formally been ceded by Turks to Greece & therefore we took it as Turkish territory no doubt squaring the elusive Greek! Not a difficult matter here I am told as nobody loves the Greek. Timeo Danaos &c.[2] We moved up to the head of the bay & dropped anchor at a place called Mudros. On the right are the Australian & New Z camps, where men come to rest & convalesce from Gallipoli in front the French camp & away to the left that of the Canadians

Friday SEPTEMBER 24

Lemnos

We are still gazing at the shore & trying to make as much of the place as our eyes & glasses can show us. It seems a dreary waste of sun scorched sand & today it was driving in clouds worse than the Borve shore in a gale.[3] The place is a vast hospital for dysentery of which there is an amount in Gallipoli, caused by bad water flies & dust. We haven't been able to get ashore yet & there are no wherrymen as at Malta & Alexandria to transport us. It seems a state of desperate confusion. Away to the right is the Arragon[4] the palatial residence of the General Staff who are living riotously clad in purple

1. The wars, between Turkey and an alliance of Greece, Bulgaria, Montenegro and Serbia, began in 1912 and ended in August 1913.

2. *Timeo Danaos et dona ferentis* (I fear the Greeks, though they bear gifts; lit. I fear the Greeks and they/those bearing gifts) – Virgil *Aeneid* ii. 49. Fr Cameron uses the word 'squaring' here in the sense of paying back.

3. A township on the west side of Barra, facing the Atlantic.

4. *Recte* Aragon. The former South American luxury liner HMT Aragon, anchored in Mudros harbour, housed the Allies' Supplies and Communications Staff. It was generally despised by the troops.

Saturday SEPTEMBER 25

At Lemnos

& fine linen. Had Mass & general Communion this morning as usual. We went ashore for a route march the ships boats being unswung & rowed by our own men. We landed at the French camp & walked along the shore. I do wish I had brought my camera. We struck a Greek village. A small church Greek at one end. Couldnt get in but it looked very filthy. Women at the well fed by a small stream & some very filthy kids. We struck off not caring to enter the village & sat on a knoll above it. Curious houses living rooms above outside stairs & cattle below. On the ridge a series of wind mills. Grain a sort of barley. Marched through Australian lines to beach.

Sunday SEPTEMBER 26

At Lemnos. Hot.

We had one last Mass on board today. Well attended 120 at HC. A fine sight. The others had none. We left the ship at 2.15 in two small steamers. Ours carrying 1st LS & RAMC & BHQ was a S Western steamer turbine "SS Sarnia".[1] She carried a gun fore & aft. We had a great send off while steaming down the lines of ships in the great harbour of Lemnos. Saw the SS Sydney with a party of tourists who looked like Americans & gave us a great cheer. All men have packs except C.O & self who are not obliged. About 7.30 we sighted Gallipoli & the line of ships bombarding the T trenches. One could see the shells bursting over the ridge of the entrance to the Dardanelles. We moved slowly up with the gathering darkness towards the beach. A steam pinnace

Monday SEPTEMBER 27

Hot

flashed up & told us to move round the torpedo nets. Round we went & put in to the shore where we anchored & awaited devel-

1. The other was SS Abassieh.

opments. In about an hour a lighter came along.[1] Men tumbled in. Was told to wait the next & take charge of HQ stuff Landing rotten. Sliding plank. Poor old Pocock knocked over. Scene on the beach stores &c. most amusing. This was 2 am. Awful confusion. Marched up with fatigue party & stumbled on the Brigade HQ. Firing going on ahead & snipers bullets whipping around. Men wonderfully quiet & cool. Most of us dazed by novelty. Allison tumbled out of pyjamas & showed us our line of Reserve Trenches for the night. We flung things down & Bowhill Paterson Campbell Robson & self tumbled into a dug out. Got a waterproof sheet & stretched out overcoat over me. Fitful sleep. Night chilly & awoke about 6am to find millions of flies buzzing. Ordered to remain there till night time. Shells One man sick. Great fun. Tea &c.

Tuesday SEPTEMBER 28

In reserve trenches[2]

Last night was unique. Part of our lot went up to the Rgt & myself Pat & 20 men went to the shore to see about baggage & stores. Started at 7.15 pm & just then a most infernal fusillade broke out in front. Star shells going up, bombs & shrap dropping & an incessant crackle of rifle & M.G. fire. Bullets whistling over our heads. Our boys got the news of French success & started cheering. Turks got jumpy & began to let off encouraged by a few rounds from us. Got safely down & found our wonderful Pocock had collected & arranged everything neatly. He is a marvel, evolving order out of perfect chaos. Got our baggage loaded onto Indian carts led by native Indian drivers. Pocock swore at them in Hindustani & got up to our Regt lines 1½

1. A shallow draught boat, often flat bottomed, used for carrying personnel or goods to and from larger ships; commonly known as a 'beetle'.

2. The Lovat Scouts were in the Reserve Trenches from 28 September until the night of 5 October. Night fatigue duties there included unloading and carrying ammunition and stores, bringing in rations, digging trenches. Work continued through the night, with a half-hour break at midnight. The Reserve Trenches were close to the Salt Lake.

Wednesday SEPTEMBER 29

miles up through the snipers. No casualties but bullets very disconcerting. Met Dr Roberts at dump & thought I was home again. Got into his half completed dug out & turned in & slept peacefully under about a foot of head cover. Turks began to shell us hard & in the evening we had a man Sutherland shot in the head by shrapnel. Dressed him with Dr & my hands were smeared over with his brains. Curiously enough he was quite conscious & sensible. Sent for Padre Lee, & got him away to F.D.S. Diarrhoea beginning to worry us. It begins that way & ends in Dysentery. Have a holy horror of shrap but curiously don't mind rifle fire although the latter is more deadly. We are just now in what are called rest trenches.

Thursday SEPTEMBER 30

Rest Trenches

These are called by the above term, & I wonder why. We are constantly catching it hot no great rifle fire but shrapnel regularly morning & evening. Went to the beach to bathe,[1] & it was ripping, with the risk of crossing the open. Got back & was met by a messenger who came for me with the news that poor Roberts was wounded by shrap. Found him bandaged, but in nape of neck a neat flesh wound but he will do. Called away to F & F trenches to a man Maloney RC shot through back. Got there & found he had been sent to Clearing Station. Saw Roberts to beach & came back with party sniped at all the time. Found young Ewan Macintyre from F.A. in my dug out. He is a change to Roberts. Poor Tommy I miss him but he was

Friday OCTOBER 1

a curious card, & he was asking for trouble. One must not

1. This was very important for the men, to minimise the spread of infection due to the flies, corpses, open latrines and rubbish dumps.

take any undue risks here. Cant say where Tommy went for once aboard the Hospital ships he is lost to our ken. Three fellows hit at the well today fetching water. This is a dangerous game as the Turks have the range of the wells to a nicety & just wait till a nice crowd collects when they let off. Had another bathe today along with Adj who seemed to be in the deuce of a funk about going through the open. Of course it is absurd but we always are absurd. The beach was like Blackpool full of naked Tommies wallowing in sea. Away to left Turks were sending shrapnel down but nobody minded. That bath was worth the risk & he took it.

Saturday OCTOBER 2

The Dr is very bad with diarrhoea consequently took on his round Went round with Cprl, Latrine Sgt &c & dispensed advice & calomel to sick.[1] Worst case that of Capt Fraser Tytler who seemed to have had a real go of dysentery Temp 103, constant purging & vomit. Got him down to 1st F.D. Station. He wont come back, last of the F Tytlers. The Turks give us shrapnel in measured doses. We had Henderson & Jackson of the Brigade Staff along at 5 pm for tea & During the meal 16 shells were sent down to flavour the meat. H looked sick & when we told them they could now try to return he dashed out & put his foot in the tea dixie! We have few visitors at tea time.

Sunday OCTOBER 3

Managed to get in Mass this morning. Alliston, Howard & Col & a few men. Mass was a joy & the Turks only let off once.

Diarrhoea is on the increase. A lot of men are down with it. Have a touch myself & it does make one horribly miserable. The main cause I believe to be grit & sand getting into the food & water setting up irritation of the bowels.

1. Chloride of mercury, used as a purgative.

Had a sick parade with the Dr in our dug out & lashed out No 7 pills calomel mostly. Poor Bowhill C Squn got laid low & we had to send him down with diarrhoea.

Monday OCTOBER 4

Mass this morning in new dug out & got 6 to Communion. The authorities are nervous about massing men together in one spot & from what I have seen they are quite justified Still if we remain here long enough I shall be able to say Mass nearly every morning & get my boys in for H. Communion in relays of 10. Col at H. Com. Also some of H.Q. Staff. Down to the beach in the afternoon among the field Ambulances. This is the hardest job I have to do. One C of E parson has been left there but he sits on his bottom bathes & eats – all equally hard, latter particularly as has had diarrhoea. Wish he would bustle round a bit.

Tuesday OCTOBER 5

Still in Reserve Trenches. A quiet morning no shells. All A Squad got the pip.[1] Fear of diarrhoea Pte H Munro Skye absolute funk. Heavy morning roll of diarrhoea. No 7 pills all round. After dinner down to beach. Searched for Pte 1910 Grant Couldnt get him. Coming home just at 1st field D.S. a shrapnel shell exploded 20 yds from me wounding two men one a Scot H[2] & other a Lochaber boy Macdonald of ours[3] neither severe. We leave our trenches tonight for front firing line relieving SH who have been there six weeks. We march at 7.30, myself bringing up rear of centre Squad. D with stretcher bearers & RAMC nearby in case of casualties. Order get the men to flank of column, detach bearers & remove to FD Station.

1. Originally a poultry disease; used humorously for humans; upset stomach, vomiting etc.

2. The Scottish Horse, two Yeomanry Regiments commanded by their founder the Marquis of Tullibardine.

3. i.e. one of the Lovat Scouts.

Wednesday OCTOBER 6

In the firing line

We are up about the centre somewhat to the right flank below Sari Bair hill. The Turks are just 50 yds in front invisible but not at all imperceptible. No casualties among ours on the march up about 1½ miles. Two Turks crawled over our front parapet with a white rag & surrendered. Kissed hands Salaam Alech[1] Even Pococks whom they mistook for a Field Marshall! We get a new kind of frightfulness up here in the shape of a shell called a whizz bang[2] made up of H Explos. & used for short distance range. No shrapnel near us but Scot Horse boys whom we relieved must have been shifting along "the Road" for a hot lot of shells were sent down to them. Read my first letter from home one from Maggie[3] a number of times. Poor soul

Thursday OCTOBER 7

Front Line Trenches

I slept last night like a log. The FFL is a specific[4] for insomnia. I woke once as a big shell flew over us but immediately dropped off again. Cup of tea at 6.30 in bed. At [sic] went round the boys. Diarrhoea seems to be improving all round. Went to the shore today. On the way down found Padre Lee, Fife & F making himself an abode. He doesn't fancy this kind of thing at all. At the beach found Dr Tuke of the Fif & Fo The lower lines seem to be full of water there are lots of little wells made by the men in four dug outs. Here we are on the crest of a ridge projecting towards the Turks but quite exposed to cross infilading fire. Returned with medical stores

1. In correct Turkish *Selamün Aleyküm* – God's peace be with you.
2. Nickname for high velocity German shell, recently introduced.
3. I have not been able to identify Maggie, nor Liza in the entry of 29 October. By 'home' Fr Cameron seems to mean Castlebay. If so, they are probably parishioners, perhaps teachers at the local school (cf. also entry for November 9, p. 66).
4. Word used in the medical sense of a particular remedy.

at 6 pm. The Sikhs are on our right.[1] Heavy sniping all night just behind my head.

Friday OCTOBER 8

In the firing line

Nothing very great last night Lots of rifle fire from the Turks. Their shots were hitting the wall of my dug out just behind my head. They have a dead bead on this spot. Went down after Med. Ins. to Brigade HQ. Brigd.[2] ill Arranging about Mass. Saw Fr Day who is really cracked. He lives at Shrapnel Valley Piccadilly officially known as the river bed. Tried to get him to go down to the shore but he wont. They call him the mad Padre & so he is. Afternoon one of my boys Gynn from Mallaig shot in the head while on sentry. Lucky boy a scalp wound only. Will arrange for Mass in C trench[3] on Sunday. Rain awful misery tumbled into blankets & waterproofs. Got into the Gurka lines. Found them sitting x legged examining their shirts.

Saturday OCTOBER 9

In the Fire Trenches

Awful night with wind & rain. Trenches mucky & choked with thistles blown in. Got up quite all right having slept right through an alarm. About 40 Turks crawling round our front trenches. If heavy rain comes this place will be unbearable. Quiet morning, afternoon very heavy shelling, with a brand new kind of fightfulness. H.E Called down to C trenches front firing line where one of my fellows Matheson was shot across the back. He was a very indifferent kind of Catholic & all along I had a lot of worry with him about duties. He had a narrow escape. Arranged for Mass

1. Part of the 29th Indian Brigade.

2. Lord Lovat, OC Highland Mounted Brigade.

3. Trench of C Squadron Lovat Scouts. There were 3 Squadrons in each Regiment, A-C and D-F.

at 6.30 tomorrow in one of the support trenches close to the fire trench. I heard confessions of D. Squad & Head Q. After turning in had to turn out again as Major Grant & little Byrne came up from Lemnos.

Sunday OCTOBER 10

Mass this morning at 6.30 in the fire trench D Squadron & H.Q. attended but not well. No vestments but a stole over my khaki what a figure I must have cut, muddy slacks tunic covered with dirt, unshaven. Altar was an empty biscuit box. The men lay down or knelt along the trench & thus we offered up the Great Sacrifice. All the men at H Communion. There is no demonstration but the fervour is there. Luckily the guns were quiet but a few bullets were coming across the parapet & whistling over my head. I was glad when it was over as the strain on my back through stooping & on my nerves was beastly. Add to that the fact that I had passed a bad night with diarrhoea (it began suddenly) & you may imagine how far from comfortable was my first Mass in the fire trenches. A report came in from the Gurka lines near us that the Turcos were preparing to give us gas Helmets issued.

Monday OCTOBER 11

Went to beach yesterday afternoon to hunt up Vickers who had been sent down for Dys. Found him alright Met Lamont Padre of Scot Hs. Got back utterly fagged. Turks were shelling road one dropped 50 yds behind me where I had passed. When I got back found that C Squadron had one man killed, Mackinnon Skye & another wounded by a shell. Slept like the dead, & woke to find the stretcher above my head perforated.

C Squadron again unfortunate. A man Sutherland Skye killed by shrapnel in his trench. To date 54 casualties including sick in 1st Regt Went to 2nd Regt[1] lines to see Col Stirling.[2] They have

1. The 1st and 2nd Regiments, Lovat Scouts.

2. Lieut Col Archie Stirling – see also note 1, p. 56.

very nice quarters down there between us & Chocolate Hill[1] but are liable to be flooded out. Heard that poor Fr Day was ordered out of his dug out on our lines. Go down to 2nd Regt on Wednesday night & say Mass on Thursday morning there. Rained like the deuce today about 12 & the whole place a sea of mud & filth. Awful.

Tuesday OCTOBER 12

The rain dried up in the afternoon but everything was so damp However got in some sleep but have another touch of the runs Everybody nowadays inquires how the bowels are & some go as far as to compare notes on the relative colours of the excreta. Horrible but this is war. The Turks shelled the Sikhs this morning. Asiatic Ann[2] plumped down 5 HE shells about 500 yds away. They came some 12 miles from the Asiatic side of the straits. Weather is becoming perceptibly colder.

I wonder what is to happen here when rain sets in. We have had only a few showers so far & that was plenty The lower trenches are still full of water in consequence. It looks to me as though these trenches would cave in of themselves without any help from the Turk when the rains do come. Saw Lord Lovat today at beach He is seedy.

Wednesday OCTOBER 13

Had a most fatiguing day. Last night intimation given that I was to go to A beach Welsh clearing Station to meet Asst Prin Chaplain. Lee & I set off & after the deuce of a walk across Lala Baba got there. Found crowds of Padres of all kinds five of ours McCarthy, Conner, Lenahan & a new comer from Mudros all more or less seedy. Conference nil Got to Welsh Station & had a jolly lunch but everyone blue about our prospects here. Paul Hook is

1. So named by the Allies because of its brown colour. It was in the Allies' hands throughout the time that Fr Cameron was in Gallipoli.

2. Usually called 'Asiatic Annie' – a Turkish long range heavy gun that fired 100 lb shells at the Allied rear positions from the Asian side of the Dardanelles Straits.

over there but he is ill just now & I didnt see him as the walk was so far. Unearthed Fr Moth Senior RC at our beach. He is a Regular[1] & does nothing but toast in the sun & curse fiercely for coming here. We all do to ourselves but I try to do a bit where I can. The beach always gives me the blues & I am

Thursday OCTOBER 14

far happier up here with the boys. Moth told me I should come down but says he has no authority whatsoever   Seems piqued that this Asst Chaplain Jarvis has superseded him   A great deal could be done with just a little organisation & more supervision but there is none of either. I shall stay where I am. Said Mass this morning for 2nd Regt in the Mess house & slept there in Col dug out.[2] Lord Lovat ill dysentery. He left today on Hosp ship. A bad blow   Went to our ASC beach. Saw some of my boys   Had a nip from Drew & Gordon. They have had a rotten time yesterday got 32 HE shells into them & 16 this morning. We had a wireless there this morning which the Turks shelled. One dropt into a dug out & exploded burying 4 men all came out alright!!

Friday OCTOBER 15

Last night as we were at dinner called with Dr to a man on D who had been wounded while out in the open stalking somebody. He got it in the side a horrid wound but he will be alright   Not an RC. Macintyre Glenmoriston. I am moving into a new dug out this evening quite a comfortable one which Ronald (Saothair[3]) Benbecula & my man Callum[4] have dug out. Went along to the beach & sneaked some wood & cart covers   One must be an

1. Fr Moth held a permanent commission as an Army Chaplain, and as such carried the initials CF (Chaplain to the Forces) after his name (see entry for 30 October). He was invalided out of Gallipoli at the beginning of December (entry for 2 December).

2. The Colonel's dug out.

3. 'the Carpenter' (Gaelic; the modern spelling is Saor).

4. Calum was Fr Cameron's batman, the chaplain being an officer. Fr Cameron elsewhere calls him by his English equivalent 'Malcolm'.

expert thief in this region. Understand some kind of move on [forward?]. Went round A Squadron trenches & confessed the boys crawling into the little dug outs in the firing line. Made arrangements for Mass & HC tomorrow. Jolly fagged. Inside worrying me but Cheer O!

Saturday OCTOBER 16

HQ

Mass at 6 am in the Mess dugout attended by C Squadron & HQ Col seedy. After Mass passed into the A Squad. Fire trenches, stood in a recess in Communication T & said the Ritual Prayers for Communion. The boys passed before me & each in passing received It was irregular of course but absolutely necessary. After all there can be no irreverence where none is intended. Went to Ambulance to get casualty returns Got them & a jolly good lunch from Major Richardson of Scottish Horse F.A. Bad news Lord Lovat left with dysentery. Col Stirling in command of Brigade[1] Sergt Major Macdonald A Squad also gone dengue fever.[2] We are losing men but this damned dysentery is getting less with the onset of cold weather.

Sunday OCTOBER 17

Mass at 6 am 1st L.S. C Squn & HQ. & a second Mass at Col. Stirlings bedside at BHQ. I hope the Col doesn't crack like the Brigadier.[3] I am gradually seeing that it is not strength & muscle but moral staying power that counts in this business. No use worrying as to the future. That is in the Hands of God Who will give

1. Lt Col Archie Stirling had been put in charge of the whole Brigade, and promoted to Brigadier General. Major A.J. MacDonald was now made CO of the 2nd Lovat Scouts.

2. An infectious fever which came on suddenly and was excruciatingly painful, especially in the joints of the body. Though debilitating it was rarely fatal.

3. i.e. Lord Lovat.

us the strength to last out if we ask it. F Day said Mass at Shrapnel Valley for 2nd LS & F & F. Some of the latter appeared They are a rotten crew & have always been that same. There is to be an assault tonight & I am going down to Dr Lee's dressing station so as to be at hand. There may or may not be a big strafe. Hope I shant fail. Turks have been shelling hard all morning & our guns active too. Sunday is always that way. My new dug out palatial in comparison with others I have slept in.

Monday OCTOBER 18

My first strafe. Went down with party of stretcher bearers, left half with Dr Tuke (F & F) at whose station I had asked F Day to remain, took the others with me to 2nd Regt & fixed up at Dr Lees dressing Post 200 yds behind attack. Lee himself advanced to the sap head[1] & I took over the DS with an RAMC dresser. All ordinary cases to be passed down to me. Attack began at 11.45 with a sharp artillery fire from our Battery on Chocolate Hill lasting about 30 minutes. At 12.15 our fellows got over their parapets & went for the Turks who were holding a redoubt 200 yds in front. They got there bombed & bayonet the Turks & dug in. Casualties at our station 1 killed (a poor boy Macdonald from Carrbridge) & 2 wounded. Same for F & F Poor boy he was shot through the heart. Laid him out behind the trench & he was buried by Lee at dawn. None of mine hit.

Tuesday OCTOBER 19

D Squadron at Mass & H Communion. Yesterday afternoon Jimmie the Postman was hit by shrapnel on the road above the well. Hear it is a slight wound. J dreaded that road & always said his beads[2] when passing. Saw him this morning at CCS & he was at once transferred to ship. Bullet extracted from ankle. He will do well & was quite pleased. Yesterday we were heavily shelled.

1. Far end of the covered trench.

2. Prayed the Rosary.

Lying in my dug out a bullet passed through my suitcase less than 2 yds away. It will be a souvenir of Gallipoli. This afternoon again shelled. Two men hit one a scratch & the other had a bullet through the neck which lodged in the fauces[1] of lower jaw nearly choking him. He was a Benbecula boy Mac Challum Ruadh[2] Dr away & I had to stop the bleeding externally easily enough but internal was bad. Hope he pulls through. Major Forsyth Grant 2nd LS.[3] badly wounded last night while spying & died of wounds this morning. Saw Col Stirling. He is a good deal improved.

Wednesday OCTOBER 20

Had quite a quiet day. The Turks shelled a good deal but not our line. They seem to single out a particular area for chastisement every day & plump shells in. Wrote a few letters & otherwise lazed. I am most comfortable (in comparison) & am quite happy. This thing can only be worked properly by remaining with the men. A Squadron came out of fire trenches today & this evening took No 1 & 2 Troops for Confessions. Next day I will take the two other troops & that will complete the round.[4] If I can carry on like this each man can make his confession once a week &

RIP

Thursday OCTOBER 21

A Squadron Mass No 1 & 2 Troops.

also receive Holy Communion at Mass. Last night at 9 pm the first of my boys, Ron. Macdonald, Moidart was killed, bullet through the brain while standing on the firing bank in A Squad.

1. Fauces – the cavity at the back of the mouth.

2. 'Son of red haired Malcolm' – in Gaelic communities people are generally known by their patronymic and/or a distinguishing feature.

3. Lieut. Forsyth Grant, who was part of E Squadron Lovat Scouts and a Squadron of the Fife and Forfars who captured the important Ashmak Dere barricade. Grant was among the team reconnoitring the ground by night.

4. Each Lovat Scout Regiment comprised 3 Squadrons, each Squadron 4 Troops.

I was just a few yds away visiting a sick man when it happened Ranald was at Mass & H Communion on Sunday. Deo Gratias. Buried him last night in Shrapnel Valley & today informed sister. Was sniped a good deal & darent light up to read.[1] Awful job taking him down the trenches. Returned at 12 pm Turks attacked us last night great hullabaloo about 1 pm. Slept on! Terrible shelling this morning. The Turks opened up with their 75 mm one captured from French. They sent a lot of HE into C Squadron fire trench & smashed 5 fellows Happened to be near at the moment & came on the scene & joined in rescue. One man fearfully cut.

Friday OCTOBER 22

Immediately after breakfast I walked off with my batman to the Canteen which is open today for our Division After getting to Lala Baba discovered it was on A beach about 4 miles away. We set off & got some lunch at Welsh Ambulance. Padre there seedy Lenehan by name, cursing Gallipoli. Got to canteen. Great scene Lots of Tommies around grasping at stores which were dispensed by a blasphemous Sergt Major who was sick of life & had no evident reason to be. Got my goods after heaps of trouble. The Turks shelled us. No one hit Got lost & after great efforts back at 9 pm & no dinner! Shelled by our own guns. Nearly got me.

Saturday OCTOBER 23

Didnt sleep last night & felt very bad. Got up late & spent a slow day. Weather very rotten cold & wet. Now begins to pall on the men the monotony of the trenches. It doesnt I must say a bit on me but I of course am always knocking around somewhere. Found my servant ill with a Temp of 104. Looks bad. Keeping him here tonight to see if he will mend Should not like to lose little Callum who is a tip top boy. Yesterday has knocked him & no wonder. I shall never forget the lift in the Indian cart bumping over

1. i.e. to read the funeral rites.

shell holes trying to keep from being pitched out & land on back of a filthy Indian mule driver! Played out!

Sunday OCTOBER 24

Mass this morning in HQ. Not many present. Our numbers are on the wane through sickness. Poor Ian Sellar dragged in looking pretty bad. He goes to Hospital today & so does my faithful little batman Malcolm. He wasn't a bit better today & he is best away I do feel sad about him No one could have been more devoted to me than he was or more faithful. I went with Col to Field Unit today & saw Campbell who was being removed. Bryant has also gone down. The young men are not standing it!

Monday OCTOBER 25

C Squadron at Mass.

A red letter day in what I was about to call a dreary life. It is strange but it is no way dreary with me. I cant say I like it yet it has its fascination. The risks are high & I suppose that does it. Went down to hunt my batman found he had been put aboard After a lot of trouble managed to follow him. Met a C of E Padre who called me to a Newfoundland boy dying. No RC on board. Gave him L Sacraments. Strange! Found little Callum looking brighter. I had a glorious bath. Interrupted in the middle of it by news that ship was leaving. Found it untrue & returned. Glorious. Tea afterwards & visited canteen. Envious of all at Mess

Tuesday OCTOBER 26

Spent a quiet day in my dug out writing letters. Sent one of the descriptive kind to Mrs Stirling. I really must see to the 2nd Regt whom I am afraid I have rather neglected of late.

Turks left us in peace today but I cant say we did for our guns particularly Vickers gave them a fierce hammering sending round after round of shells into them. I dream of another visit to that ship. I should love a job of that kind & an RC Chaplain is badly wanted there. However there isnt enough of us. Wrote Milighan mother, Mrs Van S. & one to Newfoundland.[1]

Wednesday OCTOBER 27

Deo Gratias.

About 12 noon the Turks suddenly began to bombard our lines sending shells into us at an unprecedented rate. They seemed to burst all over us mostly HE I lay low in my dug out waiting a call or calls for I thought the Regt would be laid out. Lull in the firing & I dashed out to find Dr had been called to A fire trenches. Got there & found total casualties to consist of one man slightly wounded. An hour before one from C (Skyeman) shot through the lungs, rifle fire. Afternoon had narrowest escape of my life. Turks sent a shrapnel plump into a group of 6 of us near road when I was going to FA. Timing fuse bad. It hit ground & burst there within a yard of me covering me with dirt.

Thursday OCTOBER 28

Had to go to beach again today much against my grain for that walk through sand & mud does take it out of me. Flynn F & F whom I was after is better slightly. He was removed last night quite unconcerned. Matheson man shot yesterday still alive but no hope. Poor chap but these Skyemen are a rough uncouth stupid lot. Major Kenny very cut up & no wonder. This is the sixth fatal case in his Squadron. A has escaped very lightly. The Lochaber boys are all safe yet whatever is in store for them.[2]

Friday OCTOBER 29

Mass in D Squadron this morning. Don't feel at all well but just indigestion. Stayed at home today & wrote long letter to Mrs Stirling. Two 9 in shells dropped quite near us today. One just

1. To the family of the boy from Newfoundland who had died the previous day.

2. The Squadrons of the Lovat Scouts were recruited on a local basis. C Squadron were mainly from Skye, D Squadron from Lochaber, etc.

behind my dug out & blew an awful hole up. Gave me the shivers for the moment. Nobody hurt. A huge post came this evening five bags full for our lot. Replies to my Malta letters from Bar Maggie, Liza &c. Great relief to get some scraps of home news in this horrid land Still one must stick it & we are trying to do so bravely. It looks a hopeless task this Suvla bay push despite the optimism of home papers. How ridiculous it is!

Saturday OCTOBER 30

Went to beach this morning On the way down met body of one of Fife & F carried down. He had been shot dead on firing line. F & F have had quite a number laid out in that way. Found that Ronald MPherson & Macintyre had been sent away on ship. Poor Matheson dead Saw procession from FA to CCS The saddest sight in this cursed land, fine strong fellows being carted away rotten with sickness. Dengue or trench or Gallipoli fever has succeeded dysentery in virulence. Met Fr Moth CF & got him round to my view that he should assume command at the same time fight for official recognition.

Sunday OCTOBER 31

Said Mass this morning at 7 at Fr Days old dug out in Perth Station for 2nd Regt & Fife & Forfar five of latter turned up. It was a lovely morning & things passed quietly, all men at H Com. This afternoon Turks flung a couple of bombs or rifle grenades into A lines (support trenches). Luckily no one injured. This is eve of All Saints & our last night in the firing line for some time. We go down tomorrow to our old trenches. I am glad since it was a bit nerve wracking We have been a full month here. Blowing a gale tonight. What changeable weather it is!

Monday NOVEMBER 1

Mass at 6.30 A Squadron

This is All Saints & we had Mass perhaps for the last time, certainly for some weeks in our little chapel & Mess. Most of the boys at HC. I do feel a bit off but after all I am doing my best which really is very little. Just after Mass was over a shell whistled over our heads from the Turk.

We left at 6 & came back to our old Reserve Trenches to find them in a filthy state. The latrines even the officers reminded me of the school closets at Barra. Everyone messed where he liked among these d—— Middlesex fellows. Their Col is a cousin of Capt Round our late Adjt. Wish we still had him

Tuesday NOVEMBER 2

Reserve

All Souls Owing to the confusion of our changing quarters I couldn't say Mass. Spent the whole day clearing up the mess & getting things orderly. What pigs these former tenants were & they were newcomers. The Scottish Horse after two months of Gallipoli are at a low ebb. They have lost heavily mostly through disease. I saw the Welsh Fusiliers this evening before they left our trenches to move up to the F & F lines vacated by them tonight. These are the fellows who bolted from the Turks. Hope they don't let the Turks down on us! Slept well last night in relief from the incessant crackle of rifles & roar of bombs & guns in the firing line

Wednesday NOVEMBER 3

Had a letter from Bar yesterday & none from Maggie. The night was quiet. I have heard that the fellows who took our places found the parapets much too high & removed two rows of sand bags. They are small men & that accounts for the increased number of stray bullets which came over last night. Went to C beach with Major Grant & arranged to be taken on board the

"Canopus"[1] as soon as she arrives. Afterwards went to our A.S.C. fellows & watched the Turks shelling a transport just arrived. She was supposed to have ammunition on board. She was hit once forward & set on fire but I think got it under. Little wicked monitor[2] near us sending out fire shells. Had a nap & discussed matters.

Thursday NOVEMBER 4

Turks shelled the rear trenches of the Brigade this morning. They sent in 6 shells in as many minutes all caused by men showing themselves in groups Last night owing to same cause 2 men of 2 LS were killed. The F & F are blamed. Went down to beach in the afternoon with Gerald Maxwell who now commands his squadron. Moved into new dug out built for me this evening by Lochaber boys. The other was unutterably filthy had been previously tenanted by a lousy Q Master of Scottish Horse I had a hunt over my person as I suspected lice & found one fat one. Damn the SH they have lost their self respect & the officers are rotters. Australians started a furious fusillade at 9 pm still going on. Wonder what it is!

Friday NOVEMBER 5

Had a very quiet night after the Australians had finished their shooting & slept well. We hear that the Turks tried to rush them out four times but they held on. 4 killed & 6 wounded among the Colonials. In the afternoon went down to FA & on returning arranged for Mass tomorrow & heard confessions in my dug out The Turks are using far more HE here than they did

1. HMS Canopus, a RN battleship of *c.* 13,000 tons, armed with four 12″ guns, twelve 6″ guns and four torpedo tubes; built in 1897; took part in the naval assault at Gallipoli in spring 1915 and also the withdrawal in Jan 1916; decommissioned shortly after the war.

2. A flat-bottomed armoured craft with 14 inch guns, used to continue giving firepower after the battleships were withdrawn.

before BHQ gets a lot of it. I scarcely have met an officer yet who is not despondent & sick of this ghastly fiasco. What a muddle & a mess has been made here time only will reveal. The common saying is that the Turks have us at their mercy & don't sweep us into the sea because the Germans want us kept here until they can come to administer the coup de grace.

Saturday NOVEMBER 6

Mass this morning for C & D Squads.

After Mass went to arrange the service tomorrow for Brigade a hard task to find a suitable place. Had lunch there & heard some Major tell us of the awful hash made of the advance of the 2nd M Division from A beach across the Salt Lake. They deployed into the open in broad daylight unsupported by guns losing 1000 men. Told to take the hill over there not to mind the one beyond Chocolate Hill (Hill W) as we had shooting rights over it. Lots of rumours going about a retirement but it seems unlikely An aeroplane of ours came to the ground in the green scrub near FA. The Turks shelled it hard dropping some into FA & beach! Wonder if they nailed Padre Ross who left a little before the shindy arose. They killed one our RAMC fellows. Dont know what happened to the aviators. Rumour of our leaving increasing.

Sunday NOVEMBER 7

Two Masses today for A Squadron at 5.45 & at BHQ for Fife & F & 2nd LS. About 40 at Communion all told. Talked to Colonel MD[1] about staying at FDS so as to be mid way. He doesnt favour it so I have dropped the idea for the nonce. Turks again chased us hard with HE sending 6 in shells right & left. One very nearly got Brig Stirling in our trench. It didn't explode but dived 6 ft into ground. They are damnable things & give one the shivers. Must say I do

1. Probably Colonel Kenny MacDonald of Tote, a veteran Lovat Scouts officer from the Boer War, now CO of the 1st Regiment.

dread them. Saw the effect of one on one of the Herefords yesterday at the FDS. It killed two men at the well & blew this boys calf right out.

Monday NOVEMBER 8

Weather fine but cold at night.

Another red letter day. After breakfast Major Grant, Scott & self went aboard the Canopus which was lying off A beach. Had a great time cocktail to begin with, a wash, topping lunch & a bath in the canteen of one of the officers Paymaster Greenwood a Catholic. My word it was a treat to sit on a decent chair at a clean table & get some proper grub. Ate like a wolf. Can eat three times what I could. Visited the canteen & bought mess stores. Grant needed some whisky! Got home safely to our lines after had a topping time. K of K[1] reported coming out here. High time. Navy seem as despondent about the job as we are. Saw Fr Ritchie an Oratorian from Birmingham naval chaplain just come aboard.[2]

Tuesday NOVEMBER 9

Fine weather

Weather has been quite too delightful in the last ten days. Not at all hot but nice & sunny. Fairly quiet morning some shelling I think at our guns. Turks have managed to plant a howitzer away on our left which peppers Chocolate hill. Saw our guns replying to it beautifully. Spent the afternoon in 2nd LS & saw Willie Mackintosh. Had letters from Maggie & Katie today. Maggie got notice to quit: Young man says place is his. Lost but it is hard lines on me & above all on poor Maggie. The new man is a rotter indeed & has no doubt some advisers! However no good worrying here.

1. Lord Kitchener of Khartoum, Secretary for War.

2. Order founded in Rome by St Philip Neri in 1575 comprising independent communities of secular clergy under obedience but without vows.

Wednesday NOVEMBER 10

Slight rain misty

Said Mass at B.HQ this morning 2nd LS. Just after coming back here at 8 am a boy from D (Lochaber) was shot through head. Found him alive. Gave last rites, & went to FA after him. Wade dressed him nicely. Heard that Kitchener had come – it is time. Well he has his job cut out for him now to clean up this mess. Saw Moth again & looked up Paul Hook at 2nd Welsh. Paul is mad I think & he looks it at any rate. Welshmen all funny. A mail tonight no letter from Bar. Am writing Maggie about her situation. Turks fired on wounded led by German frightfulness.

Thursday NOVEMBER 11

Cloudy & Windy

A quiet day with us. Chocolate Hill was very heavily shelled today. They burst very high but did damage I am informed. Our reserve draft from Mudros came up under Hingston. Does not look like a withdrawal. Kitchener is here just now & the story is he is to decide which is to be advance or withdraw. I suppose we shall know in time but to me one appears just about as feasible as the other. Padre Lamont Scottish Horse FA. had a service this evening for his men in Gaelic. Wrote to Canon MD,[1] Lady Emonte & Maggie.

Friday NOVEMBER 12

Wet in morning Evening fine wet night

Went with Gerald Maxwell to FA & then on to Lala Baba where we had some food with Col Shaw Stewart who commands the 53 RFA Visited Loyd in FA. I fear he is for the ship. Drew is ill with jaundice. Little Macinnes still alive & half conscious. Watched the

1. Probably Canon Donald MacDougall, parish priest of St Margaret's, Roy Bridge, who had baptised Hugh Cameron in that parish nearly forty years before; or possibly Canon John MacDonald, parish priest of St Kieran's, Campbeltown.

artillery at work at the observation post. Most intensely interesting the duel. Below our own battery pegging away directed from where I was & Turks slinging HE's down to right of us to A Beach. The Turks have masked their guns most effectively. Had letter from Fr B Katie & Roberts.[1] No letters yet arrived from here to them at home 18th October. Feeling at home pessimistic about the war & particularly the East. Beginning to notice now.

Saturday NOVEMBER 13

Cold. Some rain.

I spent the day writing letters Wrote to Barry & to Dr Roberts at length. They wrote on the 21st October & then they had not had any letters from me. Turks shelled a lot this morning to our right. They got an officer & two men of the F & F, all wounded.
They gave us fits too in the afternoon. Went down to Fr T & heard confessions in Tukes Hosp. surgery afterwards through the Machine Gun Battery. The 2nd LS move back to the very rear lines of trenches behind us. No need to arrange for Mass for them. Had a shrapnel bullet through my canvas roof this afternoon.

Sunday NOVEMBER 14

Cold & Stormy SW Wind

Mass at 6 am for A Squad. 36 at H Communion & at 7 at BHQ for Fife & F & Machine Gun Battery 21 there. Cochrane came over. After breakfast went on board HMS "Canopus" with Scott, Miller & Capt Oldfield Had a nice bath & reception from Paymaster Greenwood & another fellow Chief Engineer These navy fellows are all extremely kind & hospitable. Lot of wind & a good sea running. The 2nd LS were all out of their trenches & got the deuce of a shelling as I was going down. Sergt Major Campbell badly wounded. Little Macinnes removed & Major Pocock gone down sick.

1. Dr Thomas Roberts, the MO of the Lovat Scouts, who had been invalided home.

Monday NOVEMBER 15

Cold. Rain & Storm

Mass at 6.30 this morning for C & D. 15 at HC. Rotten day & I feel & am rotten The dust is blowing in clouds. Sat in Major Frasers[1] dug out a moment & a shrap burst all about us. Am getting accustomed now to it all & fatalistic like everyone else. Heard on the Canopus that Kitchener landed yesterday at A beach. We may expect some developments in this rotten situation. A retreat would be as disastrous as an advance it seems to me & the weather is against our sitting tight where we are. There was a furious row for half an hour this evening. A mine was blown up at the front & away went the MGs & our artillery. It was deafening.

Tuesday NOVEMBER 16

Beautiful Weather

A great storm of lightning wind & rain last night. I managed to keep dry & slept through it all like a child. Our fellows spied a battery of Turkish guns up the valley towards Anafarta & Major Grant tried to get our guns to concentrate on the spot. F & F had 3 men wounded by shrapnel this morning one an RC Pierson to whom I was called. Saw him at C.C.S to which I went. Major Pococke seedy. Post night, one from Katie & Maggie. A horrendous artillery fire broke out again this evening. Our guns battered the Turks in trenches & the whole line was covered with the smoke of bursting shells. Attack to be made tonight by 54 Div on our Right.[2] Gas helmets to be ready. Likely night for it.

Wednesday NOVEMBER 17

Horrid weather Wind & rain

A most beastly day in point of weather. First part wind very

1. Major Hon. Alasdair Fraser, Lovat Scouts. He was one of the original Scouts from 1901.

2. The 54th was one of 7 Divisions sent as reinforcements in the summer. They were Territorial Regiments.

high which blew the dust in clouds. In the evening heavy rain & towards 9 pm the wind died down. If today is typical of what is before us Gallipoli is just hell in winter. Both sides inactive. Last night the 54th near Anzac tried to rush the sap explored the other evening but were driven back with loss. I hear they are to carry it tonight. Latest story is that for every field officer shot Turks pay sniper a certain reward but if sniper shoots any man with "red tabs"[1] he gets shot himself! Staff at a discount   Wrote to Dr Carmichael. Mouldy may rejoice that he isnt here.

Thursday NOVEMBER 18

Beautiful day cold & frosty

Went very early to beach F this morning. Pococke, Drew, Lloyd & Capt. Oldfield going on ship today. Poor old Pococke. He was very downhearted. Met Fr Moth. Hook has hooked it to Alexandria. Toothache! Also met a young Catholic Dr at Scottish Horse FA   Power. Lunched there. Afternoon looked up 2nd L.S. & found Mackintosh a bit seedy. Arranged for Mass at HQ tomorrow at 9 & collared a fellow Macmillan a backslider registered Presly, from Kintail. Turks shelled our Mess after tea, nearly got some of us. Latest Peninsular joke: Visitor being shown the islands by junior Sub   "That is Imros, Samos, Lemnos & that" indicating 'Arragon' "that is Chaos"! Great.

Friday NOVEMBER 19

Lovely morning.

Mass this morning at 9 am for 2nd L.S in reserve rear trenches   Only 8 though at Communion. Called at W Kent R[2] a few Catholics. Arranging Mass for them on Sunday. Wrote Dr Carmichael a long letter   Just after I got up to BHQ the 2nd LS lines down the communication trench got a fierce shelling from

1. Any man with 'red tabs' – i.e. a Staff Officer.

2. The West Kent Yeomanry, a part of the S.E. Mounted Brigade, which was now part of the re-organised 2nd Mounted Division.

the hill batteries. Lucky for me I had just got under cover. Afternoon I spent with Nigel Dawson of 1 Scottish Horse an RC. Met Tullibardine[1] in the trench after coming back from A.D.S. & had a long crack with him. He is a great sport. Archie Cameron walked in from Mudros!

Saturday NOVEMBER 20

Very cold but dry

Have a rotten cold on me & feel very miserable. Lee has gone down sick from the Fife & Forfar. I am thinking of joining the Ambulance on beach as there is no priest there in that line of FA except Moth who is seedy. In the afternoon went to F & F lines & across to the Scottish Horse Met a young lad there called Mullally from Glasgow RC who knew Pat Long & the others at Kelvinside. Back again for a lot of confessions at 5 pm for tomorrow. Not a grave[2] among them & that is the usual experience. No temptations the world & its attractions are gone & men are face to face with God & they realise it.

Our mails have been torpedoed & sunk! Hard lines.

Sunday NOVEMBER 21

Bitterly cold

Two Masses today first at B.H.Q. had F & F. some 2nd LS, some Scottish Horse, some REs & two Gloucesters. About 20 in all at Communion. 2nd Mass at 7.45 in 1st L.S. A Squad. 40 at communion. Cold worse & no warm underclothing. Col Macdonald[3] ill with phlebitis Hope it isnt serious enough to require his removal. It will be a bad blow to my work among 1st LS. The A is a bitter enemy I can well see & has few friends anywhere in this

1. The Marquis of Tullibardine, founder and CO of the Scottish Horse; later 8th Duke of Atholl.

2. i.e. a grave or mortal sin.

3. Kenny MacDonald of Tote; cf. n 1, p. 65.

show. Cold much worse & I feel about played out & sick of this hopeless struggle. At the same time I will try to carry on till I drop.

Monday NOVEMBER 22

Windy & very cold

One great consolation I have here is in the men. C & D turned out this morning at 7.15 for Mass & I had 30 at Communion. With my bag yesterday that means close on 100 almost all I have left. Poor fellows they are a fine lot but getting downhearted. Went down in morning to FA & made arrangements with Col Mackenzie & subsequently went to BHQ where orders were issued attaching me from tomorrow to FA until the Regt returns to reserve trenches [ ] & on the whole it is better as our new firing line is too near the Turks to admit of Mass being said with safety. Had letters from Lady E, Garnett Fr Barry & Katie. Better news from Barra.

Tuesday NOVEMBER 23

Cold

Quite suddenly at 10 am we had orders that everything about moving was cancelled, including my move to FA. Of course there is considerable excitement as to what it may mean & speculation & rumours are rife, but who knows. Archie Cameron attached to 2nd LS.

Thought we should get new orders tonight about moving but no. Rumour strong that we go out of this & it looks a bit like it as everything seemed to have been fixed up accordingly for a move & then it turned a wash out! Lord how we should all jump were it so. Heard Lovat was back in Scotland.

Wednesday NOVEMBER 24

Cold

After breakfast went down to FA & heard all kinds of yarns. Rumour has it now that we are going to Lala Baba why there chi lo sa[1] Saw Willie Mackintosh who is very seedy indeed. Lee is better. The FA cant get enough stores or building material Coming back just dodged a fire burst of shrapnel around the well & DS caused by an officer of the Devons marching down some 50 men in the open. 7 were wounded & the officer & it served him jolly well right. The Scottish Horse were also much in evidence. Lord what fools people are About 4 pm big burst of rifle fire in front lasted 10 minutes

Thursday NOVEMBER 25

Very Cold

A miserable day very cold & dull. Morning wrote some letters one to Bar one to Duncan & am writing one to Lady Emonte. Colonel a lot better but I fear very much he will go for good. Dr seedy also. Afternoon went to Scottish horse lines saw some of the boys & had tea with Major Dawson. S.H very fed up & longing to quit Had a general notice of a bombardment to begin at 5.30. It was a fiasco a few rounds fired by guns to draw Turks but they wouldnt be drawn. We are to remain here ten days, then the firing line.

Friday NOVEMBER 26

Awful night of rain.

An hour after writing last lines, orders came to send down all our kits & retain only two blankets. Great excitement. Col is ill. Now begins the misery. About 6 pm it began to rain violently Thunder & lightning a most awful night. Trenches flooded with water & the barricades erected in the river bed burst & a torrent of water swept down the communication trenches S Lane & Patmos Avenue[2] filling up the trenches & every dug out. Mine dry. Took the Col in & turned out. Most awful night. May I never see a worse. Cleared out of my dug out to admit Col Macdonald.

1. Who knows? (Italian).

2. Names used by the troops for two of the Communication trenches.

4. On the night of 26 November 1915 torrential rain flooded the watercourses above Suvla, at least one of which burst into the Communication trenches and thence down into the Reserve trenches. Over 200 men died, either drowned or frozen in their saturated clothing in the sub-zero temperatures. This picture shows a few of the 500 who survived but suffered severe frostbite, sheltering in a make-shift hut made from empty biscuit tins.

5. View from Chocolate Hill towards the Aegean Sea and the island of Samothrace. Middle foreground is the Salt Lake, dry in the summer and with the marks of wagon tracks upon it. The low hill beyond to left is Lala Baba. Chocolate Hill, so named by the troops because of its colour, remained in British hands throughout Fr Cameron's time at Suvla.

Saturday NOVEMBER 27

Rain & Blizzard

A worse day followed a bad night. Men had to get out of trenches during night & camp in the open. When daylight came they were shelled. None of ours hit some casualties among F & F. Men ordered up to firing line at 5.30. They are soaking. Havent a dry stitch on & God knows what may be. Col came down to FA & I came down with my things. Awful to see the men preparing to go,[1] but needs must I suppose Got down soaked through to FA & went to sleep as I was. Ambulance crowded.

Sunday NOVEMBER 28

Sleet. Blizzard

Awful night A blizzard of sleet & snow. How the men are God only can tell. Welsh camped on the scrub in front of us & numbers coming in half dead & some dead of exposure. In the evening lots of men & officers crowded in in a pitiable state. Ambulance crammed 200 instead of usual 50. Cant evacuate to ship owing to blizzard. May God keep us & the poor fellows in the firing line.

Monday NOVEMBER 29

Cold & Wind but Dry

Today better. Rain has ceased but temp low & freezing Cant get mens clothes dry & they live in crowds huddled together half dead with cold. Seven of the Welsh Fusiliers died of exposure today. Buried one in the afternoon Evening in the operating theatre a good number of wounded. Ambulances shelled in the morning. Dont know what it may mean but looks ominous. Keen

1. On the night of 27 November the Highland Mounted Brigade received orders to take over the front line. In the open and by night it took them two hours to get up to the front trenches. They remained there for the rest of the Campaign, the Lovat Scouts making up the final rearguard at the evacuation.

frost in the evening & calm. Heavens what a debacle. The worst has not yet come

Tuesday NOVEMBER 30

Frost Rain

Weather freezing. Very cold at night Ambulance crammed. Gerald Maxwell down today & left for Hospital frost bitten feet. Moth leaving also so I am alone here.[1] A large number of the men have frost bitten feet & will be permanently disabled if not crippled. Col Stirling came down today & he is bearing up well. Lt J Dewar[2] shot in thigh but has not yet turned up & we fear he is dead. Ambulances shelled this morning probably on a/c of crowds of men around. Welsh got tight & looted rum result seven died of exposure.[3]

Wednesday DECEMBER 1

Frosty but fine & sunny

A strenuous day for our Ambulance was crowded with patients some wounded but most frost bitten. Orders came to evacuate all who were at all bad rest to go back to duty. Major Fraser came in wounded through thigh & scrotum. Narrow shave but he may do. Went down to beach CCS to arrange about his going aboard & was shelled. Turks shelled the Hospital lighter like fun, & it was exciting here for a bit Allistair taken off at night also a lad Macmillan Mallaig I fear fatally wounded. Boys at front are better now & with improved weather should do.

1. He was now the only RC chaplain at the Ambulance line.

2. Lieut J. Dewar of Lovat Scouts was seriously wounded up at the Firing Trenches.

3. See also 29 November entry. This incident apparently occurred after a lorry was sent up to the lines with a supply of food and rum to combat the cold. Finding no-one about, the driver left the consignment, which some of the Welsh troops found and drank. Feeling themselves warm they took no care to find shelter or keep heated, some even stripping to the waist. Seven died of exposure.

Thursday DECEMBER 2

Cold Frost Sunny

A quiet day. We evacuated all our sick last night In the afternoon the Turks shelled the lighter so hard that we had to stop sending more away. Sent away all my heavy kit & am left with a few blankets Very few of the boys are in from the 1st L.S. They are standing the ordeal very well from all accounts. Not many RCs have come in. Visited Scottish Horse FA & all over Moth gone & am left alone on this line of Ambulances. Foot very painful not frost bite.

Friday DECEMBER 3

Foggy

A quiet day. In the evening & afternoon went up to the front line & visited the boys. What a change the bad weather has made Communication trenches blocked firing trenches almost as bad little or no head cover. The boys are quite well & cheerful. Called on the Brigadier Stirling & found him very fit. He is holding up well, & indeed these men are gallant fellows holding the line under conditions one could scarcely like to imagine

Saturday DECEMBER 4

Cold

Quiet day. A bit of intermittent shelling. Two men of 2nd LS brought down shot through the head. Went around to spy out Catholics & arranged to have service on CC.S. this evening 7 officers & about 200 men of the Somersets[1] invaded the 2nd Mounted Amb.[2] Nothing the matter. RMO evidently got at & there has been the very devil of a row or likely to be one. Yet these men did not come from the firing line where the conditions are much

1. The West Somerset Yeomanry, part of the 2nd S. Western Mounted Brigade.
2. i.e. the Ambulance Station of the 2nd Mounted Brigade.

worse. Between the Welsh[1] & the Somerset Yeomanry there is not much to choose.

Sunday DECEMBER 5

Fine

Had a kind of scratch service today at C.CS about 20 in all were present mostly RAMC & transport [ASC?]. Prayers sermon & a hymn. Confessions in the afternoon. Got a wire to the effect that a man Macdonald RC from Beauly was badly wounded & then another that he was dead. Went along in the evening to bury him & buried him at Oak Fire Burial ground. Had to crawl out on our faces owing to sniping fire & read a very short service indeed over the poor fellow. Got down very tired & wearied. Am developing a steady evening temperature now & feel very rotten.

Monday DECEMBER 6

Dull but fine

Yesterday the Turks suddenly opened out with their artillery & pounded Lala Baba, Chocolate Hill fiercely about 12.20. It looked like an attack at first. Result 3 killed & a lot of mates laid out. The blizzard took a heavy toll out of the hill above A beach where a number of our men were frozen stiff in their dug outs. Major Dawson Scottish Horse down ill. Turks shelled Australian FA at Anzac & 13 men were killed in one of the tents. Great excitement now as to what is to happen to our Brigade & we are having visions of Egypt.

Tuesday DECEMBER 7

Dull & Cold

Major Dawson gone. Made the round of all FA's very quiet & few in. The Turks shelled Anzac again & in the evening our ships (monitors) opened a horrendous fire on the slope below Sadi

1. The Welsh Horse, part of the Eastern Mounted Brigade.

Behr[1] & plastered the place. The enemy replied & they had to move away. Furious bombardment of Lala Baba from the ridge & our guns hard at them   Didnt notice much in the firing line & hope there wasn't any thing   Called to the 2nd Welsh FA to an RC from Derby. Mails today lots of letters from home.

Wednesday DECEMBER 8

Dull & Cold

Major Lindsay gone sick a great loss to Brigade. Brigadier is a gallant man & has held out well in face of absolute exhaustion. Furious bombardment of Lala Baba, & a number of casualties reported. Rumour of evacuation en masse contradicted today[2] but expect that 2nd Mount. Division may be cleared out somewhere. The sooner the better   None of us would be sorry to leave this damned hole of a grave yard where so many brave men have fallen in vain. Field cookers ordered to be sent away tonight. Looks promising but chi sa   No use speculating & it is as well

Thursday DECEMBER 9

Weather good

Went up in the afternoon to our lines & saw the boys who are getting somewhat fagged. The strain is telling on them. The Scottish Horse move up tonight & they & our Brigade are to fight their way down. It seems that the incredible folly of making public the intention to evacuate Gallipoli has been perpetrated. By this time the Turks have it & are preparing accordingly. Orders tonight that

1. Fr Cameron must be referring to Sari Bair (or Behr) – see Map 3.

2. This entry, and that of 9 December, suggest that clear and detailed plans for evacuation were public knowledge and had been leaked. This does not square with the received historical account, which has the Turks knowing nothing of the evacuation until it was completed. Could they in fact have heard of the plans, but either believed that they were a bluff or had been changed? Or were Fr Cameron and those with whom he mixed simply mistaken in their belief that word had reached the enemy and that they were 'preparing accordingly'?

tomorrows mail is the last. It may be the last I & many more will receive. O Lord give me the grace to do my duty like a man! I shall send this diary to Bar by one of those who go before
[added in margin] 9 pm, Violent artillery fire from our guns. Didnt draw any answering fire.

Friday DECEMBER 10

Dull but fair

me in the hope it may eventually reach him if I dont. I feel rottenly ill. In the last week I have been fighting it & trying to stick it but am afraid the end is near. Temp & rotten pulse & a touch of the skitters. Last night coming down from the firing Line felt unutterably rotten

I write this on Sunday 12 on board the Hospital ship Sarapana. I collapsed altogether on Friday afternoon & the OC came along examined me called in Lieut Mitchell result in half an hour 2.30 was shoved on board the ship Nice ward only one officer in besides myself. Lt Caldwell of the Cheshires

Saturday DECEMBER 11

Dull

Bath & bed, first time I have been in sheets for three months. Had a rotten time at first. High temperature, pleurisy & a fat dose of coughing. Didnt take the slightest notice of anyone & yet I cant help feeling ashamed to have had to leave the boys. All the same I couldnt have held on another night. Everyone here most kind. Feeding good though my ration was a meagre one & ship very clean & well kept. She is BI5 [or B1G?] AC boat & was taken over by the navy when in course of construction & adapted as a Hospital ship.

Sunday DECEMBER 12

Rain

Pretty rotten yet Temp high & no sleep I just hate the nights The ward I am in is full 12 officers in ill one badly wounded. Mulcachy of the Scottish Horse came in in the morning & Geordie Middleton in the afternoon We have about 800 sick & wounded aboard & are bound for Lemnos where tranship 200. Left Gallipoli beach at 2.45 pm & I hope I may never see it again. At the same time I do feel leaving my men The last thing I noticed was a shell dropping in the water not far from one of our monitors which was giving the "Temple" a bad doing. Got into Lemnos about 9 pm & had to anchor outside

Monday DECEMBER 13

Foggy

Still seedy. Temperature keeps up. The other fellows all nearly alright. Watched the ships in Mudros. Thank heaven we are not being dumped here. Saw a transport full of troops entering the harbour.

Left Lemnos at 1.45 pm bound for Malta. It is a toss up whether we will be sent straight home or be unloaded at Malta & I am going to leave the matter alone Still too bloody sick to care, guts head chest joints everything all going together. Had about 6 calomels so far no explosion

6. Fr Cameron, photograph probably taken in Castlebay when he was parish priest at Our Lady Star of the Sea, c. 1910.

MEMORANDA[1]

OCTOBER 6[2] (written in Peninsula)

I am minded to jot down my impressions of Gallipoli acquired & gained after 6 weeks fighting or rather in the midst of the fighting How do we stand as a regiment or Brigade, our own little lot who landed here on the 26th Sept raw soldiers & may now be classed as veterans Losses in numbers. We have now lost 400 men 300 by disease 100 by wounds 25 per cent. Yet we have fought in no action worth speaking of. At that rate this Brigade[3] would be extinguished as a fighting force by Xmas. Yet in comparison we have stood the test well. The Scottish Horse came to Suvla three weeks before us 3000 strong. They have lost / now ⅔ of their total & are below three figures.[4] The English Yeomanry came out on the 10th August fought their way in that awful muddle in broad daylight to Chocolate Hill lost 1000 men. Three weeks ago they hadnt enough men to do guard & are off to Mudros a mere disjointed handful. Yet since the 10th Aug there has been no general action & a division on this sector has been practically melted away. Whats up? Just disease. Dysentery for every man killed or wounded four at least have gone down by sickness. It is damnable for a bit of common sense feeding would have prevented it to a great extent. Men have been fed / here in an Eastern climate as they were at home. Bully beef & biscuit is the badge of the Army at home & here, & bully beef is here a most damnable concoction for mens guts whatever it may prove to be elsewhere.

1. New pages in the original are marked with a /
2. *Recte* 6 November.
3. i.e. the Highland Mounted Brigade, of which the Lovat Scouts formed a part.
4. He clearly means below 1000.

Then men are kept hard at work digging & carrying who ought to be in Hospital. It is hard on an OC to see his unit melting away & not enough sent from home to replace the wastage. But it is bad for the nation to have their best men killed off here when they could have been saved to fight elsewhere.

Bad generalship is the next thing. This is for my own use & I can put my thoughts down for they are the thoughts of the whole of us. From start / to finish Gallipoli has been a most abominably managed business. Had the fine material available been properly handled we should long ago have been in Stamboul instead of holding three miles of a flat dominated on three sides by the Turkish guns. We were up on these heights more than once & bad leadership in high places lost them to us. That is what makes the temper of the Army so bitter. As I write there seems to be an awakening at home as to the true facts Wounded men are sent home & these men will speak. I hear that General Munro[1] has scrapped the famous Arragon the rendezvous of the incompetent Generals / who feast in fine linen every day in absolute security & send men to rot or be killed in this damned hole which provides them with a safe & lucrative job. What about men who sent troops in broad daylight across the Salt lake to Chocolate Hill when they could have got there safely at night as it was in our hands; 1000 men were lost. What about the system which allowed it. One of the RAMC fellows was met by a Brigadier in charge of a Brigade with an inquiry as to where exactly the Turks were placed! What he answered I dont know, probably waved them towards Achi Baba.[2] Finished Nov 12th. Havent changed my opinion. On the contrary!

/ The events of Nov 26th & the three days which followed have proved conclusively that we cannot expect to hold the plain during the winter months. Suvla is simply a mud flat most of which is at the most a foot or so above sea level. The trenches cut across it

1. *Recte* Monro. Gen Sir Charles Monro, who succeeded Sir Ian Hamilton.

2. Achi Baba, away down near Cape Helles.

are about 6 ft deep There is no natural drainage along the flat & no attempt whatever at trench drainage has ever been made. The engineers do not seem to have made a great show of skill What about digging long communication trenches from the rear into the front line at the Ashmak Dere On the night of the 26th there was very heavy rain lasting about 4 / hours. The river came down & very naturally poured down these trenches flooded out every dug out & finding no outlet down by BHQ stayed there! The usual lack of forethought of course. What will happen when the rainy season does come on as it is said to come on in January we can never realise. The whole plain will be an extension of the salt lake which is already rapidly extending past Chocolate Hill towards the Dere. It will be impassable for the trenches cut across will fill up & be a nice set of traps to drown people in. For the life of me I cant see how we can / hope to hold the plain. The Turks cant either but they may get Chocolate Hill. If we have to retire we shall precisely be where we were when we landed here for the first time in August What of all the thousands who have perished by death wounds & disease! The politicians at home, Bottomley[1] foremost say hold on. Well I do wish the whole damned crew of them were planted here for a single week to carry out the holding on! This is pessimistic but I have been a pessimist almost from the start about this venture & events have justified me. Dec 9th I have heard now there is to be a general / evacuation besides the plain.[2] On this flank the HMB & Scottish Horse are to be the rear-guard & behind each comes a stretcher bearer party from each Ambulance so that we are literally the last If I am allowed I shall make one of that last party. It is sad but it was inevitable The Turk has not thrashed us we have been beaten & driven from Gallipoli by the incompetency & idiotry of our higher command, & no

1. Horatio Bottomley, financier and journalist, creator of the magazine *John Bull*, who profited from a number of lucrative enterprises set up by himself in connection with the war.

2. i.e. apart from the troops on the plain at Helles.

name seems to be too base to apply to Ian Hamilton[1] & the crowd of imbeciles by whom he surrounded himself & wasted time, & who were foisted into commands for which they were unfit by the demi-mondaines[2] & petticoats of London society!!

1. Fr Cameron's total condemnation of Sir Ian Hamilton is not entirely in tune with the view of most historians, who admit his failings – lack of decisiveness, leadership and judgment – but also recognise his strengths – integrity, intelligence, charm, sensitivity and personal courage. Clearly such qualities, the shortcomings and even perhaps some of the strengths, fitted him ill for Gallipoli; as one recent commentator has put it, 'asked to play Henry V at the Dardanelles, he turned in a memorable Hamlet'.
2. The word is a late 19th c. French coinage, meaning women of high social standing and doubtful reputation.

7. Fr Cameron, now a Monsignor and Provost, grey haired and less slim than of old, photographed *c.* 1931 when in his last parish, Our Lady & St Columba's, Kingussie.

INDEX

also available from Mungo Books

A Record of Generous People

A History of the Catholic Church in Argyll & the Isles

John Watts

'This is an important work ... thoroughly researched but very readable. I warmly recommend it.'

Rt Revd Joseph Toal
Bishop of Motherwell (former Bishop of Argyll & the Isles)

This is a history of the Catholic Church in the Western Highlands and the Islands of Scotland, where the Catholic Church has an unbroken tradition stretching back one and a half millennia. Part One presents a summary of the Church through the years 500–1878, and Part Two a more detailed account of the modern diocese of Argyll & the Isles (1878 to the present).

The author has made extensive use of primary sources – contemporary manuscript and printed documents and correspondence, including those held in the Diocesan archives – as well as newspaper reports and (for the later chapters) personal interviews.

The story is told chronologically, introducing key events and people, and exploring themes such as the deep spirituality of the West Highlands and the Isles, their great contribution to the Church nationally, the problems of small size and remoteness, etc.

The book chronicles a long, unique and living tradition. And while the author has honestly recorded the harm sometimes done to the Church both from without and within, the story that he tells is nevertheless not only positive and affirmative but one of which the Catholics of the Western Highlands and the Islands can be justly proud.

ISBN 978-1-905965-11-3

A Cairn of Small Stones

John Watts

'An exceedingly well framed novel ... [with] immense feeling for the land and its people. A scholarly work, but written by a man too informed to be patronising, too compassionate not to leave his reader with a sense of magic of [the] glen and the strength of its people.'

The Catholic Times

ISBN 978-1-905965-00-7

Eilein na h-Òige

The Poems of Father Allan McDonald

Edited by Ronald Black

'A very valuable mine of information on Father Allan and Catholic Gaeldom.'

Abbot Mark Dilworth OSB

The name of Father Allan McDonald (Maighstir Ailein), 1859–1905, is renowned in the Gaelic-speaking islands of Uist, Barra and Eriskay. A native of Fort William, he wore himself out in the service of his parishioners at Daliburgh, and was transferred in 1894 to Eriskay, his beloved Eilein na h-Òige ('Isle of Youth'). Among his works was the publication of a Gaelic hymnal which the editor has combined selections of in this volume with twenty-seven poems, providing a resulting body of some sixty items with an English translation, introduction and notes.

ISBN 1-901157-61-X

available from Ovada Books

To Heal the Broken Hearted

The Life of St Charles of Mount Argus

Paul Francis Spencer CP

'Anyone interested in the life of St Charles, this holy man, will find this book inspiring and helpful. He represents the ideal of a humble, holy and dedicated priest.'

Father Benedict Groeschel CFR

For almost thirty years St Charles was visited daily by hundreds of people who came to Mount Argus in Dublin to receive his blessing and to be prayed over for physical, emotional and spiritual healing.

This biography reveals Charles' own inner struggles through which he learned compassion and understanding for others. Removed from Dublin for a time 'because of his extraordinary cures', he was until the end of his life subjected to criticism and humiliation, even within his own religious community. Crippled by constant pain in his later years, he continued to devote his life to the poor, the sick and the needy.

His life exemplifies that fusion of action and contemplation which was intrinsic to his vocation as a Passionist. Following the teaching of St Paul of the Cross, Charles centred all his prayer and activity on the Mystery of the Cross. His life manifests his deep awareness of the profound link between the Crucified Christ and the crucified ones of our world.

Paul Francis Spencer CP, edited *Dear Brothers & Sisters: Letters of St Charles of Mount Argus to his Family* (Ovada 2014) and translated with Martin Coffey CP *In the Heart of God: The Spiritual Teaching of St Paul of the Cross* (Ovada 2008). In 1994 his work *As a Seal Upon Your Heart: the Life of St Paul of the Cross, Founder of the Passionists* was published by St Pauls.

ISBN 978-1-905965-02-1

MUNGO

Mungo Books is an imprint of Ovada Books focusing on books of Scottish Catholic interest. Ovada Books has as its aims the promotion of Catholic faith and culture and helping people to understand the Catholic Faith through publishing, retailing and other means.

If you would like to join our mailing list and receive our free biannual newsletter of Passionist spirituality, *Ovada*, or would like further information on how you can help our work, please contact us at:

info@ovadabooks. com

ovadabooks.com